Postgraduate Handbook

A Comprehensive Guide for PhD and Master's Students and their Supervisors

https://doi.org/10.21775/9781910190753

Aceme Nyika

Graduate Support, Research and Innovation Department
University of Pretoria
Pretoria
South Africa

Caister Academic Press

Copyright © 2018

Caister Academic Press
Norfolk, UK

www.caister.com

British Library Cataloguing-in-Publication Data
A catalogue record for this book is available from the British Library

ISBN: 978-1-910190-75-3 (paperback)
ISBN: 978-1-910190-76-0 (ebook)

Description or mention of instrumentation, software, or other products in this book does not imply endorsement by the author or publisher. The author and publisher do not assume responsibility for the validity of any products or procedures mentioned or described in this book or for the consequences of their use.

All rights reserved. No part of this publication may be reproduced, stored in a retrieval system, or transmitted, in any form or by any means, electronic, mechanical, photocopying, recording or otherwise, without the prior permission of the publisher. No claim to original U.S. Government works.

Cover design adapted from Figure 5.2.

Ebooks

Ebooks supplied to individuals are single-user only and must not be reproduced, copied, stored in a retrieval system, or distributed by any means, electronic, mechanical, photocopying, email, internet or otherwise.

Ebooks supplied to academic libraries, corporations, government organizations, public libraries, and school libraries are subject to the terms and conditions specified by the supplier.

Contents

	Preface	v
1	Factors to Consider When Deciding to Obtain a Postgraduate Qualification	1
2	Philosophical Background of Knowledge and Some Adult Learning Theories: Simplification of the Terminology	9
3	Postgraduate Programmes: Variety, Depth, Credits and Enrolment	19
4	What is Research? Research Questions, Research Designs and Types of Variables	27
5	Reliability and Validity of Quantitative Research Instruments	39
6	Writing a Research Proposal: From Title Through Research Question and Conceptual Framework to Methodology	49
7	Postgraduate Thesis, Dissertation or Research Report: Different Formats and Flow From Title to Conclusion	69
8	Research Integrity: The Obvious and the Less Obvious Dimensions	79
9	Professional Doctorate Degrees: How Do They Differ From Conventional PhD Degrees?	93
10	'Guys! Let Me Tell You About My PhD Supervisor': Postgraduate Supervision Practicalities and Approaches	97
	Index	109

Current Books of Interest

DNA Tumour Viruses: Virology, Pathogenesis and Vaccines	2018
Pathogenic *Escherichia coli*: Evolution, Omics, Detection and Control	2018
Enteroviruses: Omics, Molecular Biology, and Control	2018
Molecular Biology of Kinetoplastid Parasites	2018
Bacterial Evasion of the Host Immune System	2017
Illustrated Dictionary of Parasitology in the Post-genomic Era	2017
Next-generation Sequencing and Bioinformatics for Plant Science	2017
The CRISPR/Cas System: Emerging Technology and Application	2017
Brewing Microbiology: Current Research, Omics and Microbial Ecology	2017
Metagenomics: Current Advances and Emerging Concepts	2017
Bacillus: Cellular and Molecular Biology (Third Edition)	2017
Cyanobacteria: Omics and Manipulation	2017
Foot-and-Mouth Disease Virus: Current Research and Emerging Trends	2017
Brain-eating Amoebae: Biology and Pathogenesis of *Naegleria fowleri*	2016
Staphylococcus: Genetics and Physiology	2016
Chloroplasts: Current Research and Future Trends	2016
Microbial Biodegradation: From Omics to Function and Application	2016
Influenza: Current Research	2016
MALDI-TOF Mass Spectrometry in Microbiology	2016
Aspergillus and *Penicillium* in the Post-genomic Era	2016
The Bacteriocins: Current Knowledge and Future Prospects	2016
Omics in Plant Disease Resistance	2016
Acidophiles: Life in Extremely Acidic Environments	2016
Climate Change and Microbial Ecology: Current Research and Future Trends	2016
Biofilms in Bioremediation: Current Research and Emerging Technologies	2016
Microalgae: Current Research and Applications	2016
Gas Plasma Sterilization in Microbiology: Theory, Applications, Pitfalls and New Perspectives	2016
Virus Evolution: Current Research and Future Directions	2016
Arboviruses: Molecular Biology, Evolution and Control	2016
Shigella: Molecular and Cellular Biology	2016
Aquatic Biofilms: Ecology, Water Quality and Wastewater Treatment	2016
Alphaviruses: Current Biology	2016
Thermophilic Microorganisms	2015
Flow Cytometry in Microbiology: Technology and Applications	2015

Full details at www.caister.com

Preface

This postgraduate handbook is intended for postgraduate students and their supervisors. As postgraduate studies are more dependent on self-directed active learning than on teacher-driven passive learning approaches, it is critical for one to know clearly why one wants to embark on postgraduate studies. This is because in general, postgraduate programmes are aimed at moulding postgraduate students into resourceful people who can think critically and can work independently. Having a clear motivation for undertaking postgraduate studies tends to have a bearing on the level of dedication and personality attributes of individual postgraduate students. The first chapter therefore focuses on reasons why one may want to pursue postgraduate qualifications.

In order to make an informed decision in terms of choice of postgraduate qualification to pursue, it is necessary to know the different types of postgraduate studies that are offered by various institutions of higher learning. Clarity of what postgraduate studies are is important because sometimes there is confusion which leads to wrongful exclusion or inclusion of some students as postgraduate students. For instance, at some universities some programmes meant for postgraduate students may leave out students studying for postgraduate diplomas yet they are actually postgraduate students. Therefore, the book gives a comprehensive overview of types of postgraduate programmes.

One challenge that is experienced by many postgraduate students is ability to successfully complete postgraduate studies within the stipulated periods for specific programmes. Some postgraduate students drop out, others fail and others take a prolonged period of time to complete their studies. There are various factors that could be attributed to failure to complete or long completion periods, and in most cases it is due to a combination of a number of factors. One of the major factors is lack or inadequacy of research skills, data analysis skills and writing skills not only on the part of postgraduate students, but on the part of supervisors as well in some cases. The book covers topics related to research methodologies, writing skills and student–supervisor relationships.

Factors to Consider When Deciding to Obtain a Postgraduate Qualification

Aceme Nyika

Graduate Support, Research and Innovation Department, University of Pretoria, Pretoria, South Africa.

Correspondence: nyikaa@yahoo.com

https://doi.org/10.21775/9781910190753.01

Abstract

As national economies across the world are increasingly becoming knowledge-driven, it is imperative that people should equip themselves with educational qualifications that are important in their fields of specialization. Whereas a few decades ago it was probably adequate to have an undergraduate degree, nowadays competition for jobs is getting so tight that postgraduate qualifications are becoming a necessity. Consequently, most countries are making concerted efforts to encourage their citizens to continue with their education beyond undergraduate level. This article unpacks some pertinent factors surrounding postgraduate qualifications and highlights the importance of developing a clear roadmap before embarking on postgraduate studies.

Introduction

Whereas undergraduate studies are structured in such a way that the learning process is driven to a large extent by the courses that are run by lecturers, in postgraduate studies the responsibility to drive the process of learning increasingly shifts from the lecturers to students themselves as the students progress from the lowest to the highest levels of postgraduate studies. In addition, research skills are considered to be important in some postgraduate studies. Consequently, a profound understanding of the philosophical underpinning of research is critical for the development of resourceful and innovative researchers through postgraduate programmes.

It is critical for postgraduate students to know why they want to obtain postgraduate qualifications and to have clear understanding of the postgraduate programmes that they intend to embark on in terms of (i) appropriateness to the students' objectives of undertaking the studies, (ii) requirements to be fulfilled by the students and (iii) feasibility in light of circumstances of individual students.

Why consider obtaining a postgraduate qualification?

There are various reasons or objectives for obtaining postgraduate qualifications depending on one's circumstances and/or passion in life. Reasons for obtaining postgraduate qualifications include:

- enhancement of prospects of getting a job;
- enhancement of chances of being promoted;
- strengthening of innovative capabilities;
- sharpening of entrepreneurial skills;
- passion for knowledge and personal fulfilment;
- 'killing' time;
- compelled to study by parents or guardians;
- compelled to study by employer.

Factors to consider when choosing a postgraduate qualification

It is important for one to choose an appropriate postgraduate programme that will meet one's needs and is suitable for one's circumstances. To be able to do so, one should first think through one's career goals and the career path that one wants to follow in order to achieve the goals. Various pertinent factors have to be considered when choosing a postgraduate qualification to pursue and they are outlined below.

Taught postgraduate qualifications: most appropriate for careers that do not require research skills

These are postgraduate programmes that are composed of taught courses only without research projects. The programmes are aimed at equipping learners with knowledge, concepts and skills through intensive modules and courses taught by educators. However, for some programmes hands-on practicals are included in order to equip learners with certain practical knowledge or skills. For instance, a programme in the science field may include practical laboratory sessions which are done as part of the taught courses. Similarly, a programme in the field of IT may include practical sessions in the computer laboratory.

If one wants a career that does not depend on research skills but is mainly dependent on subject knowledge and certain skills then an accredited taught programme that is not entirely based on research may be the most appropriate. For instance, if one is interested in a career that is mainly dependent on computer programming then a taught postgraduate qualification that focuses on computer programming could be appropriate. If one would like to be a radiographer then a postgraduate programme that equips learners with the skills and knowledge needed by radiographers would be appropriate.

Research-based postgraduate qualifications: most appropriate for careers that require research skills

These qualifications are based entirely on research projects. In other words, research contributes 100% of the credits required for the qualification. Thus, the final write-up of the research project conducted is what is examined. The final write-up is a thesis if it is a doctorate degree qualification, a dissertation if it is a master's degree qualification or a research report if it is a postgraduate honours degree or postgraduate diploma qualification. Whereas master's degrees may be by coursework, by research work or by a combination of coursework and research project, doctorate degrees are generally by 100% research work.

Although taught courses may be taken during the course of study, the courses do not contribute any credits to the qualification. Taught courses may be taken if they are deemed critical for certain skills or knowledge that underpin the research project. Thus, taught courses may be taken to facilitate conduction of the mandatory research project but they are not mandatory *per se*. For an academic career, research-intensive postgraduate programmes are very useful, and a path that includes master's degree by research and PhD degree could arguably be considered to be the standard route.

Taught plus research postgraduate qualifications

Some postgraduate programmes have both taught and research components which contribute credits towards fulfilment of the requirements of the qualifications. The proportions of the components may vary from one programme to another and from one institution or country to another. However, for most taught plus research programmes the taught component generally contributes at least 50% of the requirements. The most common proportions of taught component to research component are (a) $50:50$, (b) $60:40$, (c) $70:30$ and (d) $80:20$.

Professional postgraduate qualifications

Unlike the other postgraduate qualifications, which are generally considered to be academic qualifications, professional postgraduate qualifications are centred on a practical component which is specific to a particular field or area of specialization. Consequently, one of the entry requirements for most professional postgraduate qualifications is that one must have a certain minimum number of years of practical on-the-job experience in the field in which the intended postgraduate professional qualification is to be obtained. The requirement for relevant experience is usually in addition to the usual requirement to have a relevant undergraduate qualification.

Academic postgraduate qualifications could be considered to be aimed at contributing knowledge to a specific discipline, whereas professional postgraduate qualifications could be considered to be focused on application of knowledge in a specific field. However, there is an overlap between the two types of qualifications because academic qualifications can cover theoretical knowledge as well as knowledge about application of theories and concepts, while theoretical or conceptual knowledge is generally required for one to be able to apply knowledge. If one is already in a certain profession and has gained experience then a professional postgraduate qualification such as a professional doctorate degree could be the most appropriate.

Modes of delivery

There are several modes of delivery of postgraduate programmes that have been developed and are being used by institutions of higher learning (Smith *et al.*, 2006). The modes of delivery include face to face, flipped classroom, problem-based learning, work-based learning, e-learning, distance education and blended learning.

Face to face

The conventional face-to-face method of delivery is arguably still the main mode of delivery, especially in parts of the world where access to internet is still limited. The face-to-face method involves didactic delivery of knowledge through lectures given to large groups of learners, tutorials, practicals, assignments and independent study.

Flipped classroom

This mode of delivery reverses the conventional face-to-face approach by enabling learners to access the lecture material in advance of the face-to-face session so that learners can go through the lecture material and have time to reflect on it before the contact session. During the contact session, the learners can ask the educator to elaborate any areas they may not be understanding. That way, contact time is used to enhance comprehension rather than to make didactic presentation of the lecture. In light of the increasing numbers of university students and hence the increasing sizes of classes, flipped classroom could address the challenges of inadequate time for learners to ask questions as the lecture materials and other reading materials are delivered in advance (Fakhr and Khalil, 2016; Flores *et al.*, 2016; Johnston, 2017).

Mechanisms of enabling access to the lecture materials vary depending on the institutional resources available. Video recordings of the lecture can be made available online. If video recordings are not possible, power point slides as well as any relevant reading materials can be made accessible online or they can be emailed to the learners. If it is not possible to make the lecture material accessible electronically, hard copies of the presentation and relevant reading material can be provided to the learners in advance.

Problem-based learning

The starting point in a problem-based mode of teaching is the presentation of a problem relevant to the field of study so that learners unpack the problem using relevant theories and concepts with the guidance of the educator. It therefore means that at the end of the learning activity learners are supposed to have grasped the pertinent theories and concepts as well as comprehension of how the theories and concepts can be applied to solve problems. The problem can be a hypothetical one or it can be a case study that may be based on real-life scenarios. Various institutions of higher learning have adapted problem-based learning as one of delivery methods used for teaching and learning (Walliser *et al.*, 2016; Moro and McLean, 2017; Okyere *et al.*, 2017).

Work-based learning

This approach is similar to the problem-based learning except that a real-life problem existing at a work place is used instead of a hypothetical one. This mode of delivery is commonly used for some professional qualifications. For instance, some health-related postgraduate qualifications are offered in conjunction with some teaching hospitals so as to enable work-based learning that depends on real-life scenarios and real-life patients in the hospitals. Some agriculture-based qualifications may involve exposure to actual agricultural activities in the field. Similarly, some business-related postgraduate programmes may incorporate work-based aspects that are done in companies or organizations.

Work-based learning brings together three stakeholders or players, namely the learner, the academic institution and the employer (Foster and Stephenson, 1998). Proper and efficient co-ordination and management of work-based learning programmes is critical for the desired quality of graduates produced to be achieved (Burdett *et al.*, 2017).

e-learning

The advent of the internet has given rise to e-learning which uses the internet as a platform for delivery of academic programmes (Brahler *et al.*, 1999; Collings and Pearce, 2002). However, it has been reported that successful completion of online courses is affected by various factors, which include lack of some important critical skills on the part of learners (Levy and Ramim, 2017), user-friendliness of the technology used for deliver and quality of subject information (Al-Samarraie *et al.*, 2017).

Distance education

The main characteristic of this mode of delivery is the absence of or very limited contact between the learners and the educators. The pedagogical materials are prepared by educators and the materials are sent to the learners physically as hard copies or electronically. In addition, other technologies such as web-based mechanisms of enabling access to the materials are now being used (Dede, 1996).

Blended learning

This method of delivery combines the conventional face-to-face method with technology-based e-learning methods (Munezero and Bekuta, 2016; Chen *et al.*, 2017). Blended learning has been described as one of teaching and learning approaches that have great transformative potential when used at institutions of higher learning (Garrison and Kanuka, 2004). Students' satisfaction with courses delivered through blended learning has been shown to be influenced by various factors which include (i) students' achievement goals, (ii) instructor expertise, (iii) instructor support and (iv) quality of the learning management system in terms of design and functionality (Diep *et al.*, 2017).

Accreditation

Before embarking on any postgraduate programme, it is important to verify that it is properly accredited by the relevant national educational authority. All academic postgraduate programmes should be accredited regardless of whether they are offered by a public or private institution. A qualification that is not accredited is not recognized by employers, professional bodies, academic institutions and other national or international stakeholders, which renders it useless.

Requirements to be fulfilled in order to graduate

Different postgraduate programmes have different requirements to be satisfied before one can be awarded the qualification. It is important to know the details of a full postgraduate programme before enrolling for it. For instance, the minimum credits that are required, whether there will be a research project or not, the courses or modules that constitute the programme, the sequencing of courses or modules and the mode of delivery (i.e. face to face, online, blended, etc.). Some academic programmes incorporate a stipulated period of 'attachment' to companies, organizations, community or some kind of field work. Such details are important for planning purposes.

Feasibility in light of circumstances of individuals

Feasibility of enrolling and completing a postgraduate programme should be considered right from the beginning. A holistic and comprehensive plan should be mapped out upfront. It may be necessary to create time to gather the pertinent facts and information first before embarking on a chosen postgraduate programme.

Full-time or part-time postgraduate programmes

Most institutions of higher learning offer some postgraduate qualifications on a full-time or part-time basis. In general, part-time candidates are given more time to complete a postgraduate programme than full-time candidates doing the same programme. This is because part-time students have employment-related commitments in addition to their academic studies. For instance, a full-time programme may have compulsory face-to-face components run during week days which some part-time students may not be able to attend due to commitments at work. Thus, some academic activities of part-time postgraduate programmes may be done on weekends or after working hours.

Tuition fees and other costs

Affordability of tuition fees should also be assessed upfront, because failure to pay the fees halfway through a programme may prevent one from successfully completing the programme. Other related costs to cover such pertinent needs as books, research projects, laptops or computers, stationary, accommodation, commuting, and subsistence should also be taken into account.

Time management

Once one has decided to study for a postgraduate qualification and has enrolled for the programme, it is very important to manage one's time properly right from the beginning. Some students tend to study without any milestones and timeframes until a few months before the end of the study programme. Such delayed time management plans do not help because the workload will have accumulated to such high levels that quality of learning may be compromised, which could lead to failure in worst-case scenarios.

A study plan for the whole postgraduate programme should be developed as soon as details of the content and structure of the programme are known. The plan should be based on the intended completion period. For instance, if a postgraduate programme is to be completed within 2 years, then the plan should fit into the 2 years with details of what should be accomplished in each of the 2 years and in each of the 24 months.

References

Al-Samarraie, H., Teng, B.K., Alzahrani, A.I., and Alalwan, N. (2017). E-learning continuance satisfaction in higher education: a unified perspective from instructors and students. Stud. High. Educ. *2017*, 1–17.

Brahler, C.J., Nils, S.P., and Johnson, E.C. (1999). Developing on-line learning materials for higher education: an overview of current issues. Educ. Technol. Soc. 2(2), 1–12.

Burdett, J., Burdett, J., Barker, S., and Barker, S. (2017). University students in the workplace strategies for successful industry placement experiences. Development and Learning in Organizations: An International Journal 31(1), 15–18.

Chen, A.K., Dennehy, C., Fitzsimmons, A., Hyde, S., Lee, K., Rivera, J., Shunk, R., and Wamsley, M. (2017). Teaching interprofessional collaborative care skills using a blended learning approach. Journal of Interprofessional Education & Practice *8*, 86–90.

Collings, P., and Pearce, J. (2002). Sharing designer and user perspectives of web site evaluation: a cross-campus collaborative learning experience. Br. J. Educ. Technol. 33, 267–279.

Dede, C. (1996). The evolution of distance education: Emerging technologies and distributed learning. Am. J. Distance Ed. *10*(2), 4–36.

Diep, A.N., Zhu, C., Struyven, K., and Blieck, Y. (2017). Who or what contributes to student satisfaction in different blended learning modalities? Brit. J. Educ. Technol. 48(2), 473–489.

Fakhr, N., and Khalil, N. (2016). Large Classroom Predicament Resolved: Tackk and Socrative in the Flipped Approach. In Conference proceedings. ICT for language learning (p. 52). libreriauniversitaria. it Edizioni.

Flores, Ò., del-Arco, I., and Silva, P. (2016). The flipped classroom model at the university: analysis based on professors' and students' assessment in the educational field. International Journal of Educational Technology in Higher Education, *13*, 21–28.

Foster, E., and Stephenson, J. (1998). Work-based Learning and Universities in the UK: a review of current practice and trends. High. Educ. Res. Dev. *17*(2), 155–170.

Garrison, D.R., and Kanuka, H. (2004). Blended learning: Uncovering its transformative potential in higher education. The Internet and Higher Education 7(2), 95–105.

Johnston, B.M. (2017). Implementing a flipped classroom approach in a university numerical methods mathematics course. Int. J. Math. Ed. Sci. Technol. *48*, 485–498.

Levy, Y., and Ramim, M.M. (2017). The E-Learning Skills Gap Study: Initial Results of Skills Desired for Persistence and Success in Online Engineering and Computing Courses. In Proceeding of the Chais 2017 Conference on Innovative and Learning Technologies Research (pp. 57E-68E).

Moro, C., and McLean, M. (2017). Supporting students' transition to university and problem-based learning. Medical Science Educator, 1–9.

Munezero, M.D., and Bekuta, B.K. (2016). Benefits and challenges of introducing a blended project-based approach in higher education: Experiences from a Kenyan university. Int. J. Ed. Dev. Using Inform. Commun. Technol. *12*, 206–212.

Okyere, G.A., Okyere, G.A., Tawiah, R., Tawiah, R., Lamptey, R.B., Lamptey, R.B., Oduro, W., Oduro, W., Thompson, M., and Thompson, M. (2017). An assessment of resource availability for problem based learning in a Ghanaian University setting. Quality Assurance in Education 25, 237–247.

Smith, A., Ling, P., and Hill, D. (2006). The Adoption of Multiple Modes of Delivery in Australian Universities. Journal of University Teaching & Learning Practice, 3(2). Available at: http://ro.uow.edu.au/jutlp/vol3/iss2/2

Walliser, J., Jigena, B., Muñoz-Perez, J.J., Pozo, L., and García Gómez de Barreda, D. (2016). Problem Based Learning: a tool to improve maritime safety learning in the Merchant Maritime University degrees. Available at: http://rodin.uca.es/xmlui/bitstream/handle/10498/18307/Maritime%20safety%20learning%20INTED2016.pdf?sequence=1&isAllowed=y

Philosophical Background of Knowledge and Some Adult Learning Theories: Simplification of the Terminology

Aceme Nyika

Graduate Support, Research and Innovation Department, University of Pretoria, Pretoria, South Africa.

Correspondence: nyikaa@yahoo.com

https://doi.org/10.21775/9781910190753.02

Abstract

Learning at university level involves learners, educators and support staff who should collectively create an institutional environment that is conducive to student-centred learning. As the core activities of universities are centred on knowledge, it is critical for all stakeholders to have broad comprehension of the main philosophical underpinnings of knowledge. The philosophical basis of knowledge should be understood in terms of the various worldviews that exist and how the different worldviews have a bearing on the approaches through which teaching, learning and construction of knowledge can take place effectively. In general, teaching approaches, research capacity, characteristics of learners and the environment in which teaching, research and learning take place affect the quality of education at universities. Academic researchers should have clear understanding of the philosophical background they want to base their studies on because it has a bearing on methodological approaches to be taken and interpretation of results thereof. However, complex terminology used can compromise comprehension of critical philosophical concepts. This article therefore explains in very simple terms the meaning of some pertinent philosophical jargon such as ontology, epistemology, axiology, research paradigms and some adult learning theories.

Introduction

There are different perceptions of what reality is, which leads to different ways of determining what is real or not real. Different worldviews are shaped by a combination of multiple factors, which include inborn characteristics, experiences, value systems, belief systems, culture, settings, etc. Historical philosophers have coined up several terminologies which have become universally accepted and are used widely in the academic field. It is therefore critical for one to understand the terminologies in order to comprehend deliberations and discourses pertaining to knowledge and learning theories. This article will therefore explain in simple terms various terminologies that are commonly used in philosophical arguments and discussions. The terminologies include metaphysics, ontology, cosmology, epistemology, axiology, research paradigms, empiricism and rationalism. The article also simplifies some adult learning theories that are commonly referred to in academic articles.

Metaphysics

Aristotle, one of the most renowned philosophers, coined the term 'metaphysics' which deals with the nature of existence and the world. The term was arguably derived from two Greek words, 'meta' which means 'after' and 'physica' which means 'physics'. Thus, the term metaphysics literally means 'after physics' which refers to the study of existence and the world beyond physical things. Metaphysics can be divided into ontology and cosmology.

Ontology

Ontology refers to worldviews of what reality or truth is. One worldview is that there is one objective reality that exists, and researchers strive to find out that reality or truth. This ontological view claims that reality or truth is not value-laden and can thus be generalized. According to this 'objective' worldview, reality exists *a priori* to any human knowledge or perception of it. An opposing ontology is of the view that reality is the human conceptualization or perception of what reality or truth is, which means that it is subjective as it depends on conceptualization/perception of individuals. It follows therefore that there can be several realities or truths, and all of them may be correct in different contexts. This conceptualization or perception-based ontology is sometimes referred to as epistemological ontology. This ontology postulates that reality is value-laden; which means that there are acceptable levels of subjectivity that depend on value systems, beliefs and other pertinent contextual circumstances.

Cosmology

Cosmology is the study of the physical origins and evolution of the universe. The modern field of cosmology that has evolved brings together the fields of observational astronomy and particle physics. The evolution of the field has been influenced to a large extent and arguably by the 'Big Bang Theory' which uses mathematical formulas and models to explain the origin of the universe (Linde *et al.*, 1994; Das, 2017). However, the theory has been debated in the context of theism (belief in the existence of a supernatural God or Gods who created the universe) and atheism (not believing in the existence of God or Gods) (Craig and Smith, 1993).

Epistemology

In simple terms, epistemology is the nature of knowledge, its sources and methods of acquiring it. The two main methods of acquiring knowledge are empiricism and rationalism (Reichenbach, 1948; Hjørland, 2005). Empiricism focuses on experiences as the basis for acquiring knowledge, hence the knowledge is acquired a posteriori, meaning after the experience. On the other hand, rationalism focuses on reason or ideas, hence it is possible for knowledge to be acquired a priori, meaning before any experience.

Axiology

The term axiology is derived from two Greek words, 'axios' which means value or worth, and 'logos', which means logic. Axiology is the philosophical study of societal values from ethical/moral or aesthetical points of view. The main ethical theories are consequentialism, utilitarianism, deontology, teleology and social contract. The theories are explained succinctly below.

Ethical or moral values

- Consequentialism is based on the notion that the moral value of an action should be assessed on the basis of the consequences of the action. In other words, if an action results in good consequences, then the action is morally right and if it results in bad consequences, then the action is morally wrong.
- Teleology postulates that if the intended purpose is right then an action is morally right regardless of the consequences which may be good or bad.
- Utilitarianism stipulates that an action is morally right if it is useful and it benefits the majority. This theory emphasizes that an action should be considered ethically right if it maximizes benefits for the majority of intended beneficiaries.
- Deontology is a theory premised on duty and rules and stipulates that one is obliged to act according to relevant rules. Thus, the moral worthiness of an action should be assessed on the basis of whether it was done according to the relevant rules and norms or not.
- Social contract theory posits that individual members of a particular society have some 'unwritten agreements' with the society in terms of how they should behave and relate with each other. The theory covers moral aspects of society in the context of political governance and how societies may have to strike a balance between individual human rights and overarching authority of the state over individual rights.

Aesthetic values

Aesthetic value refers to the nature of beauty attached to nature, culture or art. Aesthetics is therefore based on emotional values that are derived from sensory perception of the beauty of nature, culture or art. The emotional values and perceptions of beauty may vary from one person to another as well as from one community or society to another.

Research paradigms

Research paradigm is a worldview, an underlying belief system or philosophy of research that guides researchers in terms of methodological approaches to be taken to answer specific research questions (Haase and Taylor Meyers, 1988). Research paradigm includes any premises and assumptions that shape a particular worldview, belief system or philosophy. The research paradigm helps the researcher to develop appropriate theoretical and conceptual frameworks that form the overall framework within which the research is to be conducted. The main paradigms that underpin research are positivism, post-positivism, interpretivism, constructivism and pragmatism. Fig. 2.1 shows research paradigms for quantitative and qualitative research.

Positivism

Positivism is based on the notion that there is universal absolute truth or reality and researchers aim to find it through quantitative research methods that are designed to prove or disprove specific hypotheses stated upfront (Idowu, 2016). Positivism is based on critical realism which postulates that reality is independent of observers, which implies that reality exists even if we may not know about its existence. Positivistic research paradigm begins with a hypothesis which is then tested deductively. In general, research methodology based on positivism is aimed at identifying and explaining relationships or causes that affect outcomes so as to formulate laws that can be generalized. Thus, positivism is the basis of quantitative research which relies on quantitative data that are collected and analysed in order to answer specific research questions through testing null hypotheses against corresponding alternative hypotheses. The null hypothesis states that whatever is being observed is due to chance, in other words, there is no difference between or among whatever is being investigated. On the other hand, the alternative hypothesis states that there is statistically significant difference which is not due to chance.

Interpretivism

Interpretivism postulates that there is no absolute truth or reality but several truths/realities that depend on context. It means that interpretivism is based on relativism, which is the worldview that different people perceive reality differently; hence, it is subjective as opposed to being objective. In contrast to the positivistic paradigm, interpretivistic research paradigm aims to develop hypotheses or theories from data. In other words, there is no *a priori* hypothesis but data are collected and then analysed inductively in order to develop theories. Interpretivistic paradigm is the foundation of qualitative research.

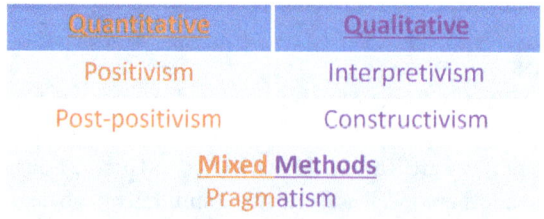

Figure 2.1 Research paradigms for quantitative and qualitative research methodologies.

Through interpretivistic research, knowledge can be constructed from the analysis and interpretation of data. Knowledge derived from the research is constructed jointly by the research participants and the researchers.

Post-positivism
Unlike positivism, post-positivism is premised on the notion that although there is absolute truth or reality, there is no single universal truth or reality (Panhwar *et al.*, 2017). Although post-positivism postulates that there is absolute reality, it acknowledges that the ability to know reality with certainty is limited. In other words, post-positivism is based on the notion that learning and gathering of knowledge are processes aimed at getting to the actual truth or reality, but the processes and observations are fallible to different extents.

Constructivism
The theory of constructivism posits that learning should be through active construction of knowledge by the learners themselves. This theory, which was founded by Piaget and is sometimes referred to as 'Piaget's constructivism', emphasizes that a learner builds structures of knowledge called schemata which are continuously amended as the learner is exposed to new experiences and or information (Ackermann, 2004). It is the continuous changes of the schemata that constitute learning. In other words, learning involves building of knowledge on the basis of what is already known by the learner and new information or experience. Pre-existing schemata may be extended or changed by the individual learners themselves, which means that they transform themselves by actively constructing 'new' knowledge (Biggs and Moore, 1993). Thus, the learner has to play an active role in learning processes rather than passively 'receiving' knowledge from educators. It means that educators should not only use traditional instructivistic methods of teaching which posit educators as the primary agents of learning who 'transmit' knowledge to the learners.

Social constructivism
The two main founding proponents of this theory were Vygotsky and Papert (Palincsar, 1998; Ackermann, 2004). The social constructivist perspective on adult learning is that construction of knowledge is not merely a cognitive process that depends on the processing of information by the brain but is a learning process that is also shaped by social and cultural factors (Palincsar, 1998). It means therefore that knowledge is constructed through the interaction between the mental cognitive processes and social reality in which the individual lives. Although both Vygotsky and Papert were social constructivists, they differed in terms of their views on the nature of the social context. Vygotsky considered the social context to be mediated predominantly through language, whereas Papert considered actions to dominate social context.

Pragmatism
Pragmatism is a combination of positivism and interpretivism and is the basis of *mixed-methods* research which involves both quantitative and qualitative research designs. Abductive strategies are used to analyse and interpret data so as to generate evidence-based

explanations of the phenomena being researched and to develop new hypotheses or theories (Carter and Little, 2007).

Empiricism and rationalism
Empiricism is the view that the only or best way to gain knowledge is through empirical data obtained from 'tangible' observations, measurements and sense experiences. In general, such empirical data are quantitative, hence positivism incorporates empiricism. On the other hand, rationalism considers reason and intuitions to be important for processes of acquiring knowledge. Interpretivism incorporates rationalism through use of qualitative data that may not necessarily be 'tangible'.

Research approaches
Depending on the research paradigm chosen to answer a research question, research approach can be deductive, inductive or abductive. The different research approaches require different data collection and analysis methods, hence it is critical for researchers to have clear understanding of the research paradigm and research approach to be used in the intended research. The different research approaches are explained in the following sections.

Deductive research approach
A deductive research approach starts with a research hypothesis, which is based on the research question. Data collection followed by data analysis is then done in order to prove or disprove the hypothesis. The data collection procedures depend on the research designs that are appropriate for the research questions to be answered. Deductive research approach follows very structured processes and sample sizes have to be of certain minimum sizes determined statistically. In general, probability sampling techniques are used and samples used have to be representative of the specific target population being studied and big enough for the findings to be generalizable to the target population. The research designs are quantitative. Fig. 2.2 shows the deductive research approach which is also referred to as the 'top–bottom' research approach.

Inductive research approach
Unlike a deductive research approach, an inductive research approach starts with data collection followed by data analysis. The analysis of data then leads to formulation of theory propositions which may eventually be developed into validated theories. Non-probability sampling techniques are used and the samples can be small without being necessarily representative of the target population being studied. The research process is not very structured and is generally qualitative. The inductive research approach, which is also referred to as the 'bottom-up' research approach, is shown in Fig. 2.3.

Abductive research approach
Abductive research approach combines deductive and inductive research approaches in order to answer a research question. The combination of the two research approaches can be done sequentially, starting with either deductive or inductive approach, or it can

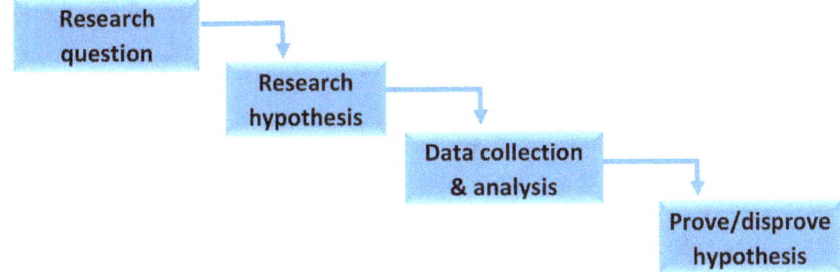

Figure 2.2 Deductive (top–bottom) research approach.

Figure 2.3 Inductive (bottom-up) research approach.

be done concurrently (the two approaches done simultaneously). As deductive research approach is for quantitative research design and inductive research approach is for qualitative research design, it means that abductive research approach is for mixed-methods research design.

Adult learning theories

The way adults learn has been shown to be different from the way children learn. Generally, postgraduate candidates are adults; hence adult learning theories are applicable to the way they learn. Relevant adult learning theories include the behaviourism theory, cognitive learning theory, constructivism and transformative learning theory. The theories are explained below.

Behaviourism theory

The behaviourism theory is hinged on a premise that learning involves stimuli and responses to the stimuli leading to changes in behaviour after repeated stimuli response cycles (Delprato and Midgley, 1992). The stimuli either suppress or promote certain responses, and if reinforced over a period of time, a particular type of behaviour develops. Although postgraduate students may indeed respond in certain ways to various stimuli ranging from the influence of their supervisors through enforced institutional management policies to socio-economic forces, behaviourism on its own cannot adequately explain the way students learn. Other intrinsic as well as extrinsic factors also influence the learning processes.

Cognitive learning theory

Unlike the behaviourism learning theory which is premised entirely on extrinsic factors, the cognitive learning theory postulates that the brain plays a major role in learning through processing of information and storing the processed information in memory. The main founding proponents of the cognitive learning theory are Jean Piaget and William Perry (Fosnot and Perry, 1996). The theory explains learning as a passive and intrinsic mental process which is affected by the developmental stage of the learner (Tennyson and Rasch, 1988). Piaget posited that cognitive development from childhood to adulthood has four main stages: (i) the sensorimotor stage during which children depend on their innate instincts and emotions, (ii) the preoperational stage (up to about 7 years old) when children become able to make sense of concrete concepts, develop differentiated emotions, understand language and make sense of real things around them, (iii) the concrete operational stage which is from 7 to 12 years old during which children develop logic but only in the context of concrete objects and events and (iv) the formal operational stage (which starts from adolescence to adulthood) during which ability to relate concepts, events and reality at abstract levels without being limited to tangible objects or events develops (Tennyson and Rasch, 1988; Fosnot and Perry, 1996).

At postgraduate level, students should be in the formal operational stage of cognitive development. However, it is not only intrinsic factors that have a bearing on the learning of students, extrinsic factors also influence learning. Consequently, Perry posited that extrinsic factors such as socioeconomic conditions, culture and religion have potential to affect the cognitive processing of information by the brain (Fosnot and Perry, 1996). In addition, Perry argued that cognitive development does not necessarily occur in clear-cut stages as postulated by Piaget, but that it involves taking of positions that continue to change under the influence of intrinsic and extrinsic factors. Perry posited nine possible positions, the major ones being duality, transitional, multiplicity and commitment.

Duality assumes knowledge and morality to be either wrong or right and true or false. Transitional positions mean that the learner takes into account many different dynamic factors and hence keeps changing his/her position or point of view accordingly. The multiplicity position is a relativist position that accepts that knowledge and morality are not absolute but depend on context. The commitment position means that even though a learner takes into account multiple points of views, the learner will want to be identified with or committed to specific knowledge or morality positions.

Transformative learning theory

The transformative learning theory captures the personal and socio-cultural dimensions of adult learning which collectively lead to development of an individual (Mezirow, 1997; Dirkx, 2000; Merriam, 2004). The theory stipulates that when an adult encounters new knowledge or new skills, the internalization process that follows should involve cognitive processing and critical reflection in the context of one's experiences, mastered concepts, value systems, beliefs and assumptions (Merriam, 2004). Thus, the frame of reference for the adult learning has cognitive, social, emotional and spiritual dimensions (Boyd and Myers, 1988; Mezirow, 1997; Merriam, 2004). The main goal of transformative learning is development of an ability to think independently and rationally.

Characteristics of the learner

There is a distinction between knowing and the process that leads to knowing which is referred to as 'being and becoming' or 'coming to know' (Barnett, 2009). According to Barnett (2009), 'being and becoming' is analogous to a journey which leads to a destination while knowing is analogous to arrival at the destination. Overall, the author argues that it is the process of travelling in the journey that is more important than the arrival at the destination. In other words, being and becoming is more important than knowing.

There are two dimensions of a learner which have a bearing on his or her 'being and becoming', namely dispositions and qualities. These dimensions are referred to as epistemic virtues. Barnett (2009, p433) defines dispositions to be 'those tendencies of human beings to engage in some way with the world around them' and argues that they 'furnish a will, of various kinds' (Barnett, 2009, p433). Five examples of kinds of dispositions mentioned are (i) 'a will to learn', (ii) 'a will to engage', (iii) 'a preparedness to listen', (iv) 'a preparedness to explore, to hold oneself out to new experiences' and (v) 'a determination to keep going forward'.

Dispositions manifest themselves through certain ways which constitute qualities of the individual person. Examples of qualities include 'courage, resilience, carefulness, integrity, self-discipline, restraint, respect for others, openness, generosity and authenticity' (Barnett, 2009, p434). Although dispositions are 'universal', qualities may differ from one discipline to another in terms of priority. For different academic and professional fields, there can be different mixes of dispositions and qualities. Thus, whereas for one discipline openness may be one of the most important qualities, for another discipline it may be resilience. For instance, although sympathy/empathy is very important in the medical field, it may not be so important in other fields such as engineering.

References

Ackermann, E.K. (2004). Constructing knowledge and transforming the world. In Tokoro, M. and Steels, L. (Eds). A learning zone of one's own: sharing representations and flow in collaborative learning environments. IOS Press, Amsterdam, Berlin, Oxford, Tokyo, Washington DC.

Barnett, R. (2009). Knowing and becoming in the higher education curriculum. Stud. High Educ. 34, 429–440.

Biggs, J., and Moore, P. (1993). The Process of Learning. New York, Prentice Hall.

Biggs, J. (1999). What the student does: teaching for enhanced learning. High Educ. Res. Dev. 18(1), 57–75.

Boyd, R.D., and Myers, J.G. (1988). Transformative education, Int. J. Lifelong Ed. 7, 261–284. https://doi.org/10.1080/0260137880070403

Carter, S.M., and Little, M. (2007). Justifying knowledge, justifying method, taking action: epistemologies, methodologies, and methods in qualitative research. Qualit. Health Res.17, 1316–1328.

Craig, W.L., and Smith, Q. (1993). Theism, Atheism and the Big Bang Cosmology. Oxford University Press. https://doi.org/10.2307/2186006

Das, T. (2017). Origin of singularity in Big Bang theory from zero point energy. Can. J. Phys. https://doi.org/10.1139/cjp-2017-0015

Delprato, D.J., and Midgley, B.D. (1992). Some fundamentals of B.E. Skinner's behaviorism. Am. Psychol. 47(1), 1507–1520.

Dirkx, J.M. (2000). Transformative Learning and the Journey of Individuation. Available at: http://files.eric.ed.gov/fulltext/ED448305.pdf (accessed 29 August 2016).

Fosnot, C.T., and Perry, R.S., 1996. Constructivism: A psychological theory of learning. Constructivism: Theory, perspectives, and practice, 2, pp. 8–33.

Haase, J., and Taylor Meyers, S. (1988). Reconciling paradigm assumptions of qualitative and quantitative research. West. J. Nurs. Res. 10, 128–137.

Hjørland, B., 2005. Empiricism, rationalism and positivism in library and information science. J. Document. 61(1),130–155.

Idowu, O.E. (2016). Positivism versus Interpretivism: Fire-war on the Methodological Approach in the Study of Organisational Culture. International Journal of Human Resource Studies, 6(4), 178–187.

Linde, A., Linde, D., and Mezhlumian, A. (1994). From the big bang theory to the theory of a stationary universe. Phys. Rev. D 49, 1783–1826.

Merriam, S.B. (2004). The role of cognitive development in Meziro's Transformational Learning Theory. Adult Ed. Q. 55(1), 60–68.

Mezirow, J. (1997). Transformative leaning: Theory to practice. New Directions for Adult and Continuing Education, 74, 5–12.

Palincsar, A.S. (1998). Social constructivist perspectives on teaching and learning. Annu. Rev. Psychol. 49, 345–375. https://doi.org/10.1146/annurev.psych.49.1.345

Panhwar, A.H., Ansari, S., and Shah, A.A. (2017). Post-positivism: and effective paradigm for social and educational research. IRJAH, 45(45), 253–259.

Reichenbach, H. (1948). Rationalism and empiricism: an inquiry into the roots of philosophical error. Philos. Rev. 57, 330–346.

Tennyson, R.D., and Rasch, M., 1988. Linking cognitive learning theory to instructional prescriptions. Instr. Sci. 17, 369–385.

Postgraduate Programmes: Variety, Depth, Credits and Enrolment

Aceme Nyika

Graduate Support, Research and Innovation Department, University of Pretoria, Pretoria, South Africa.

Correspondence: nyikaa@yahoo.com

https://doi.org/10.21775/9781910190753.03

Abstract

It is critical for prospective postgraduate students to have a broad understanding of the variety, scope and depth of postgraduate programmes so as to firstly make informed choices before enrolment and secondly be able to develop a well-thought-out study plan for the whole postgraduate programme. In simple terms, a postgraduate qualification is a qualification that is obtained by a candidate who has already graduated with a first degree. The first degree is generally referred to as an undergraduate degree and is the degree that one can enrol for after successfully completing secondary school education. This articles gives a detailed explanation of various postgraduate programmes offered by institutions of higher learning across the world, entry requirements, notional hours of study, credits and grading systems.

Introduction

Postgraduate programmes can be made up of 100% taught courses, a combination of taught courses and research component or 100% research work. Although different academic institutions can package their postgraduate programmes differently, they use specific credit systems to differentiate between postgraduate certificates, diplomas and degrees. Postgraduate degrees include master's degrees, master of philosophy degrees and doctorate degrees.

Honours degrees may be considered to be postgraduate degrees if they are undertaken after a first degree has already been obtained. However, some honours degrees are actually undergraduate degrees by virtue of them being undertaken straight after secondary education without having obtained a first degree. Medical and dental degrees that are obtained by medical practitioners are actually undergraduate degrees even though upon completion the graduates are referred to as 'Doctors'. This means that they obtained a medical undergraduate degree that enables them to practice as medical doctors, it does not mean that they obtained postgraduate degrees.

There are also postgraduate programmes that do not lead to degree qualifications but diplomas and certificates. The entry qualifications for such postgraduate diplomas and certificates would be a first degree, which means that without having obtained a relevant degree already one may not be enrolled for the postgraduate studies. However, there are some exceptions which enable experience in the relevant field to be considered even if the applicant does not have an undergraduate degree. Whereas a research component is considered important for most postgraduate degree programmes, most postgraduate certificates or diplomas tend to be composed of coursework only. The various postgraduate studies are explained in detail in the sections below.

Honours degrees

Undergraduate honours degree

Some universities offer undergraduate degrees as either general or honours degrees. Some universities offer 3-year general degrees with the possibility of an honours route for students who pass at levels above certain cut-off marks. For example, a student may be studying for a Bachelor of Science degree made up of chemistry, biology and mathematics in the first year. At the end of the first year, the student may be offered to pursue an honours degree in any of the three subjects depending on whether or not the student's end-of-year marks are above a cut-off point of say 75% for the particular subject. If the student is offered more than one honours route, it is up to the student to choose which subject to take up at honours level. In the third year, the honours student would have to undertake a research project on the basis of which a research report would be submitted for examination. The research report would be in addition to coursework; the degree programme is composed of coursework plus a research project. Such an honours degree would still be an undergraduate degree.

Postgraduate honours degree

However, honours degrees can be undertaken at postgraduate level. Some universities offer honours degrees that require one to have obtained a relevant first degree to be eligible. The entry requirement is usually a general degree. A candidate would have acquired a first degree already which would be used as an entry qualification for the honours degree. For instance, certain Bachelor of Science General degrees may be entry requirements for particular Bachelor of Science honours degrees, which would be considered to be postgraduate degrees. Such postgraduate honours degrees are generally 1 year for full-time students and 2 years for part-time students. The honours degree would be composed of coursework and research project. The honours degree research projects are supervised by academic members of staff, but the projects do not have to be extensive. Desk-top research projects or secondary data analysis generally suffices for honours degree purposes. The aim is to expose the honours students to the process of research, from research topic through research questions or specific objectives, methods, results and conclusion to reporting research findings.

Master's degrees

There are three main types of master's degrees: (i) master's degree by research work, (ii) master's degree by coursework and research project and (iii) master's degree by course work. The main difference between (i) and (ii) is that the masters by research work requires a more extensive research project than what is required for the masters by coursework and research project. Taught masters that are entirely based on coursework are relatively becoming rare due to the increasing recognition of the importance of research for academic and economic development.

Master of Philosophy degrees

Master of Philosophy (MPhil) degrees are considered to be higher than master's degrees but lower than PhD degrees. The MPhil degree is not a master's in Philosophy degree; it is a Master of Philosophy in any field. It could be an MPhil in a specific area in the natural sciences, social sciences or health sciences. MPhil degrees are by 100% research work. Registration for an MPhil degree can be used as a stepping stone for registration for a PhD degree at some universities. A candidate can register for an MPhil degree so as to have access to academic support to enable the candidate to develop a research proposal that is acceptable for a PhD degree programme. The candidate would then upgrade the MPhil degree programme to a PhD degree programme. It means that the candidate will eventually graduate with a PhD instead of an MPhil degree. Globally, MPhil degrees are arguably becoming less popular than master's and doctorate degrees.

Doctorate degrees

There are two main types of postgraduate doctorate degrees that are awarded by universities on the basis of examination of work submitted by candidates, namely the academic Doctor of Philosophy (PhD) degrees and professional doctorate degrees. Honorary doctorate degrees are not based on examination of work submitted by candidates but are based on recognition of outstanding contribution to specific areas of specialization. However, there are several other types of degrees which are sometimes generally and incorrectly considered to be postgraduate degrees mainly because after graduating the graduates acquire the title 'Doctor', which is abbreviated as 'Dr'. For instance, professional degrees that have to be obtained by medical practitioners before they can practice as health care providers are not postgraduate degrees, they are undergraduate degrees. Such professional undergraduate degrees include the Bachelor of Medicine and Surgery, Bachelor of Dentistry and Bachelor of Veterinary Medicine. The academic, professional and honorary doctorate degrees are explained in detail in the following sections.

Doctor of Philosophy degree

Doctor of Philosophy (PhD) degree is an academic doctorate degree that is obtained prospectively after registering through an appropriate department or school of a university that is accredited to offer the PhD degree. A PhD degree is generally offered as a structured programme composed of a research project aimed at contributing some new knowledge to the existing body of knowledge. A PhD candidate has to undertake PhD studies under the supervision of an academic staff member appointed by a relevant committee or department of the university that deals with postgraduate students' affairs. The PhD candidate has to write a thesis that is examined by internal examiners drawn from the university where the candidate is registered and external examiners drawn from other universities. In the academic field, the academic PhD is arguably regarded as the gold standard of the highest level of postgraduate qualifications.

Professional doctorate degree

The second type of postgraduate doctorate degrees is professional doctorate degrees, which are also referred to as industrial doctorate degrees. The work on the basis of which one can be awarded a professional doctorate degree is work that has already been done as part of one's professional practice or duties but is also of such high academic quality that it constitutes a significant contribution to knowledge. A proposal giving details of the work done and how the work contributes towards knowledge has to be submitted to a university and the university assesses if the work is adequate for a professional doctorate degree in terms of quality and quantity. If the proposal is accepted, the candidate then writes up the work in a thesis under the supervision of an academic supervisor appointed by the university.

The thesis would then undergo an examination process that includes internal and external examiners just like is the case with PhD degree theses. Professional doctorate degrees are generally considered to be important for professional development of professionals who are already employed, which is different from PhD degrees which are generally critical for academic development in academic environments. Thus, although the professional doctorate degree is a postgraduate degree, it is not one and the same degree as the PhD degree.

Honorary doctorate degree

Another type of doctorate degrees is the honorary doctorate degree, which is not necessarily a postgraduate degree because it is not based on academic work per se. An honorary doctorate degree is awarded by a university to an individual who has excelled in her/his area of specialization and has made a significant contribution to that area. The individual does not necessarily have to have acquired any university degree(s) to be eligible for an honorary degree. For example, a musician who has been successful and influential nationally and or internationally may be awarded an honorary doctorate degree in arts even if the musician does not have any tertiary academic qualifications.

Postgraduate diplomas and certificates

To study for a postgraduate diploma or certificate one should have obtained a degree that is in an area relevant to the diploma or certificate to be studied for. However, there may be some exceptional cases where experience may be considered in lieu of degree entry qualifications. Most postgraduate certificates are entirely taught programmes whereas some postgraduate diploma programmes may have a research component which culminates in research reports that have to be submitted for examination in partial fulfilment of the requirements for the diploma.

Notional hours and credits

Notional hours are the estimated number of hours that are needed for a learner to study certain material in order to achieve specific expected learning outcomes. The notional hours are used to determine credit points (credit weighting) as an indicator of the volume and depth of teaching and learning required to achieve specific intended learning outcomes. Notional hours include time spent on face-to-face contact teaching and learning, online learning, distance learning, tutorials, practicals, reading study materials, preparing for and writing assignments, individual study, formative assessments, continuous assessments and summative examinations. Ten notional hours are equivalent to 1 credit. Table 3.1 shows some examples of notional hours and credits for some postgraduate programmes.

Table 3.1 Examples of estimated notional hours and credits of postgraduate programmes

Postgraduate programme	Components*	Notional hours*	Credits*
Non-degree programmes			
Postgraduate certificate	Coursework (100%)	600	60
Postgraduate diploma	Coursework plus a very small project	1200	120
Degree programmes			
Honours degree	Course work plus a small research project	1200	120
Master's degree by coursework + research project	Course work plus a small research project	1800	180
Master's degree by research project	Research project (100%)	1000	100
MPhil degree	Research project (100%)	1800	180
DPhil degree	Research project (100%)	3600	360
PhD degree	Research project (100%)	3600	360
Professional doctorate degree	Previously published work (100%)	3600	360

*These are examples which may differ from one institution to another.

Levels of academic programmes

There are different systems of demarcating levels of academic programmes in different countries or regions of the world. For instance, in an effort to make qualifications obtained in European countries comparable and compatible, the European Qualifications Framework (EQF) was developed (http://ecahe.eu/w/images/3/34/EQF.pdf). Thus, qualification levels of different European countries can be referenced to the equivalent EQF levels, which is important in the selection process of candidates for postgraduate studies.

The levels of studies are in terms of the numbers and depth of constituent courses, the overall programme and the intended learning outcomes. For instance, the Framework for Higher Education Qualification (FHEQ) in England, Wales and Northern Ireland classifies first-year undergraduate studies as FHEQ level 4, second-year undergraduate studies as FHEQ level 5, third-year undergraduate studies as FHEQ level 6 and postgraduate studies as FHEQ level 7. FHEQ Levels 3 and below are for such studies as secondary school education which are below first-year university level. Thus, according to the FHEQ system, a three-year undergraduate degree is at FHEQ level 6 while a master's degree is at FHEQ level 7.

The South African National Qualification Framework (NQF) differs slightly from the FHEQ system. Secondary school education as well as further education and training are classified as NQF levels 4 and below while higher education and training studies fall into NQF levels 5 to 10. According to the NQF system, higher education and training studies include (i) national certificates at NQF level 5, (ii) national diplomas at NQF level 6, (iii) bachelor's degrees and advanced diplomas at NQF level 7, (iv) honours degrees and postgraduate diplomas at NQF level 8, (v) master's degrees at NQF level 9 and (vi) doctorate degrees at NQF level 10. Thus, according to the NQF system, an undergraduate degree is at NQF level 7 if it is a bachelor's degree or NQF level 8 if it is an honours degree while a master's degree is at NQF level 9.

Requirements for enrolment into postgraduate studies

In order to understand the requirements for entry into postgraduate studies, it is necessary to first have a look at the various undergraduate qualifications that exist so as to be able to distinguish those that may suffice as entry qualifications for postgraduate studies from those that may not be acceptable. However, there are several different routes through which one can get to postgraduate studies, and there may be different requirements from one institution to another and from one country to another. Different academic institutions may use different grading systems for the undergraduate qualifications, which may have a bearing on one's eligibility for enrolment into postgraduate studies at a different institution to that where one obtained one's undergraduate degree from.

It is partly for such reasons that some countries like the European countries and South Africa developed a mechanism of evaluating qualifications that may have different grading systems. For instance, in South Africa the South African Qualification Authority (SAQA) is an arm of government that is responsible for evaluating any qualifications obtained from non-South African academic institutions. Thus, if a candidate who obtained educational qualifications from institutions outside of South Africa wants to apply for enrolment into an academic programme offered by a South African institution, the candidate has to submit his/her qualifications to SAQA for evaluation. SAQA then issues certificates that state the equivalent South African NQF levels of the 'foreign' qualifications.

Undergraduate degree programmes

In most countries, there are two main categories of undergraduate degree qualifications, namely bachelors and honours degrees. As the honours degree is generally at higher level than the bachelor's degree, it is possible for candidates to obtain the bachelor's degree first (which is usually 3-year degree programme) and then study for a year to obtain an honours degree in the same field of study as the bachelor's degree. In such cases, the honours degree obtained after one has already obtained a bachelor's degree can be considered to be a postgraduate degree. In some cases candidates enrol for a 4-year honours degree programme which means that they obtain an honours degree straightaway without having obtained a bachelor's degree first. In such cases, the four-year honours degree is considered to be an undergraduate degree. However, another school of thought regards an honours degree as an undergraduate degree regardless of whether it was obtained after obtaining a bachelor's degree first or not.

Some professional undergraduate degrees such as medical and dental degrees take longer than the academic bachelor's degree. Although professional degrees such as the medical and dental degrees may take as long as seven years to complete, they are still classified as undergraduate degrees. Part of the seven years is used for internship which prepares the candidates for their professional duties by equipping them with practical skills.

In the USA, the bachelor's degrees are generally four-year degree programmes offered mainly by public universities. Honours degrees are not common in the American educational system. Another unique feature in the USA is another type of undergraduate degree called an 'Associate degree' which is at a lower level than the bachelor's degree. Associate degrees are offered by community colleges and private junior colleges. The associate degrees are generally focused on specific specialized areas in professional or vocational fields such as technical specialties, nursing, allied health professions and business specialties. However, there are also associate degrees in the academic field which can be used for entry into bachelor degree programmes.

Grading systems

The grading system at undergraduate level is important because grades of undergraduate qualifications are considered when applications for enrolment into postgraduate studies are evaluated. Different grading systems may be used by different institutions or by different countries but in general there are approximate equivalents across the different systems. Table 3.2 shows approximate equivalents for the 3 common grading systems in different parts of the world.

Higher postgraduate degree qualifications such as doctoral degrees are usually not graded. For doctorate degrees, the outcome of the examination process can be a pass or an outright fail. However, master's degrees that have taught components can be graded.

Table 3.2 Different undergraduate grading systems that may be used for selecting postgraduate students*

Percentages	Letters	Numbers**	Words	
			Type a	Type b
75 to 100%	A	1	First Class	First Class
70 to 74%	B+	2.1	Second Class (Division one)	Upper Second Class
60 to 69%	B	2.2	Second Class (Division two)	Lower Second Class
50 to 59%	C	3	Third Class	Third Class
0 to 49%	F	Fail	Fail	Fail

*The table shows some commonly used grading systems. However, there may be other systems that are not included.
**There is another grading system called 'Grade Point Average' (GPA) which uses a scale ranging from 0 to 4 representing 0% to 100%. A score of 2 is the cut-off point (corresponding to 50%), which means that a score below 2 is a fail.

Entry requirements for postgraduate studies

An honours degree is the minimum entry requirement for postgraduate degree studies at most institutions of higher education. Thus, a bachelor's degree may be considered inadequate for entry into master's degree programmes. Empirical studies have shown that the grade of undergraduate degree qualifications affect the opportunities available to students when they leave universities (Di Pietro, 2016). The better the classification of the undergraduate degree the higher the chances of being accepted for postgraduate studies or getting employment (Di Pietro, 2016). However, in some cases experience may be considered in lieu of an honours degree for a candidate with a bachelor's degree.

In general, a master's degree is the minimum qualification required for entry into a doctorate degree programme. However, some institutions or countries may have other specific entry requirements such as entry tests, interviews, brief research proposals and or motivation letters. For instance, American public universities consider results of the Graduate Record Examination (GRE) to be the main determining factor when selecting postgraduate students.

References

Di Pietro, G. (2016). Degree classification and recent graduates' ability: Is there any signalling effect? J. Ed. Work 30, 501–514. https://doi.org/10.1080/13639080.2016.1243230

European Qualifications Framework (EQF). Available at: http://ecahe.eu/w/images/3/34/EQF.pdf (accessed 2 July 2017).

Framework for Higher Education Qualification in England, Wales and Northern Ireland (FHEQ). Available at: http://www.qaa.ac.uk/publications/information-and-guidance/publication?PubID=2718#.WVjuThWGPIU (accessed 2 July 2017).

South African Qualification Authority (SAQA). Available at: http://www.saqa.org.za/ (accessed 2 July 2017).

What is Research? Research Questions, Research Designs and Types of Variables

Aceme Nyika

Graduate Support, Research and Innovation Department, University of Pretoria, Pretoria, South Africa

Correspondence: nyikaa@yahoo.com

https://doi.org/10.21775/9781910190753.04

Abstract

A clear understanding of what research is and the different research designs that can be used is critical for research to be conducted correctly. As there are various research designs, a researcher has to use the most appropriate one for the research question to be answered. A wrong choice of research design leads to wrong data being collected and analysed, which means that the research question cannot be answered correctly. This chapter gives an overview of research designs and types of variables that can be measured. Diagrams and examples are used to make it easy for various concepts to be understood.

Introduction: what is research?

In simple terms, research is a systematic search for factual information regarding a specific topic through systematic collection, analysis and interpretation of data. There are four broad categories of the aims of doing any research. The aim of conducting research may be to (a) better understand a specific phenomenon, (b) better understand existing problem or challenge, (c) find ways of controlling phenomenon/problem/challenge and (d) improve or invent new products or 'tools' used in various fields.

When faced with a phenomenon, problem, challenge or innovative idea that needs to be researched, the first step is for the researcher to ask a relevant question about the phenomenon/problem/challenge/innovative idea. The question becomes the research question which guides the approach (research methodology) that has to be taken to answer it. Depending on the nature of the phenomenon/problem/challenge/innovative idea to be researched, it is possible for a research question to be broken down into several research sub-questions that need to be answered first in order for the overall overarching research question to be answered. Converting the research questions into corresponding specific objectives helps to clarify what exactly is being looked for by conducting the research project.

Research question and hypothesis

A research question based on the knowledge gap that is to be addressed guides the researcher in choosing the most appropriate research paradigm and research methodology. An ideal question gives such critical information as the 'gap' in knowledge that is being investigated, the main variable(s) to be measured and the target population. Research questions can be classified into four broad categories which are descriptive, comparative, relational and causal questions. The categories are not mutually exclusive; hence a study aimed at answering a comparative question can also be descriptive. Similarly, a study addressing a relational question can have some descriptive and comparative aspects.

A research hypothesis is a proposition based on existing knowledge on the subject. Thus, it is an *a priori* position that aims to answer the research question. A hypothesis should at least state the variables that are concerned and the predicted relationship between them. The purpose of conducting the research is then to prove or disprove the hypothesis put forward upfront. However, the nature of some questions is such that it is not possible to formulate a research hypothesis because the questions are of exploratory and descriptive nature.

Descriptive research questions

Most descriptive research questions start with 'What' or 'How'. The aim is to describe a particular phenomenon quantitatively or qualitatively, depending on the wording of the question. If the question requires quantitative research, descriptive statistics are important in describing the phenomenon. Examples of descriptive statistics include measures of central tendency (means and medians), measures of dispersion (standard deviation, inter-quartile ranges) and proportions (prevalences, incidence rates, etc.). No research hypotheses can be formulated for purely descriptive research (quantitative or qualitative) because it is aimed at merely describing what is existing without comparing or relating some parameters with others.

Comparative questions

The main aim of these questions is to find out if there are any differences between two or more groups and the nature or extent of the differences. Comparative questions generally lead to observational research that is aimed at understanding existing characteristics of a phenomenon without attempting to manipulate it in any way. Comparative questions can be answered through prospective or retrospective observational research, depending of the nature of the question. For instance, one may be interested in comparing the national revenue derived from mineral resources for some specific countries over the past decade. That would require a retrospective comparative observational study.

Relational questions

This type of questions requires the relationship between certain variables to be investigated. The variables can be of the same group or they can be from different groups of participants. The relationship could be an association or correlation and not necessarily a causal one. Thus, an increase or decrease in one variable may be correlated with an increase or decrease of another variable. In terms of association, one may wonder if failed car hijacks are significantly associated with certain characteristics of vehicles such as models, security features, etc. A question about the trend of a variable or variables over a certain period of time is also a relational question. For relational questions, a research hypothesis can be formulated. In order to be able to test the research hypothesis, it should be broken down into a null hypothesis and alternative hypothesis.

Causal questions

The aim of this type of questions is to find out if one variable causes another variable or if a set of variables causes one or more variables. This type of questions requires experimental research to be conducted and it can only be done prospectively. The variable that is being investigated as a potential cause is called the independent variable and the outcome variable which is potentially caused by the independent variable is called the independent variable (the effect).

Types of research

Types of research depend to a large extent on the research aim and question(s) to be addressed because they determine how the research is to be conducted in order to be able to answer the research question(s). Unpacking the categories of aims of research given above under Introduction: what is research? helps to understand the different types of research that can be conducted. Categories (a) and (b) are different from categories (c) and (d) in terms of the approaches to be taken by the researcher. Fig. 4.1 depicts different types of research designs. The differences are explained in sections that follow.

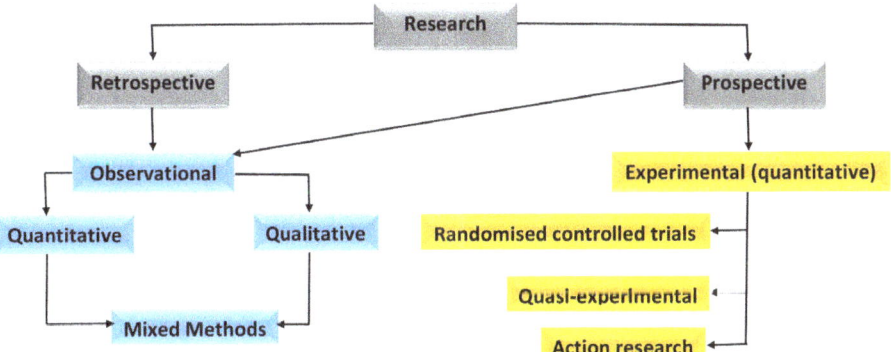

Figure 4.1 An overview of types of research designs.

Observational research

Observational research can be quantitative, which means data collected and analysed are in the form of numbers, or qualitative, which means data collected and analysed are in the form of words. Observational research can be prospective or retrospective. Prospective research means that the researchers start data collection from some current point in time going to the future for purposes of their research. Retrospective research means that researchers use data that already exist. The data may have been collected for other non-research purposes and by people who may not be researchers. For instance, data gathered during routine operational activities of an organization may be analysed at some point in future in order to figure out certain trends that may be captured by the data.

An example for category (a) is a case in which one may want to know the species of trees that are found in a particular locality. Similarly, if one wants to know the chemical and microbiological composition of water bodies that are used by a certain community, that type of research would fall under category (a). Another example is a study to figure out the characteristics of passengers that have used a certain airline over the past decade. A study conducted to find out the chemical components of soil from a particular locality would be an observational study even if the soil samples have to be analysed in a laboratory equipped with the necessary equipment. At the end of the day, the researchers would describe the chemical profile of the soil and the laboratory-based analyses would not change the chemical composition of the soil.

If there is a gradually increasing number of people presenting with diarrhoea at a particular hospital, one may want to know details about the problem in terms of the demographic characteristics of the patients, residential areas where they come from, the types of food they may have eaten before they fell ill, any events they may have participated in, any pathogens that may be detected in their stool, etc. It is important to emphasize that even if samples of stool may be taken into a laboratory to examine what type of microorganisms are there, the researchers are still merely trying to observe what is in the stool. The laboratory-based observations do not change what is in the samples of stool. Such type of research would fall under category (b).

Categories (a) and (b) would require the researcher to systematically observe and describe what is existing without any form of intervention that may change what is observed. Although the researcher has to systematically collect, analyse and interpret data, the researcher does not actively do something that may change the variables that are being measured. This type of research is called observational research. There are two broad types of observational research; naturalistic observational research and participant observational research.

Naturalistic observational research

Naturalistic observational research involves studying phenomena in their natural environments without introduction of any external factors at all. For example, if one wants to study how kudus live in their natural environment and if they 'socialize' as families and or communities, one would have to find a way of studying the kudus in their natural environment without disrupting their normal day-to-day activities and interactions. Ideally, the kudus should not even notice the presence of the researcher otherwise they may change the way they behave. The need not to disrupt the normal and natural environment makes purely naturalistic observational research difficult to conduct. For instance, a researcher who wants to conduct ethnographic qualitative research on particular aspects of a community may go and life with members of the community for a certain period of time in order to observe the particular aspects of the community. However, the mere presence of the researcher in the community may make them change to some extent the way they normally go about doing things.

When dealing with research that involves human beings, conducting purely naturalistic observational research may render the research unethical by violating some human rights of the people researched. One classical example of a naturalistic observational research project that was unethical is the Tuskegee syphilis study that was conducted in the USA from 1932 to 1972. The study was aimed at observing the natural progression of syphilis in infected black people without treating them. The study continued even after penicillin was proved to be an effective antibiotic for treatment of syphilis in 1940.

Participant observational research

If the researcher gets involved to some extent, then the observational research is referred to as 'participant observational research'. A researcher could provide a hypothetical scenario and find out how people or any other participants would react or behave. A simple example to explain this type of research is a situation where one wants to find out how people react when they come across something valuable (like money or a gold ring) within premises like a conference centre, a university or bank. One could secretly introduce a valuable item and then secretly observe what people would do.

A good example of participant observational study was conducted by Rosenhan (1973) in collaboration with seven of his colleagues. The aim of their study was to find out how diagnosis of mental illnesses was done at hospitals. The eight researchers presented themselves to various hospitals and when asked what was wrong with them they simply answered 'I am hearing voices'. They were all diagnosed with schizophrenia and they were hospitalized for periods ranging from 8 to 52 days. Thus, the researchers became so involved to the extent that they were actually the 'objects' utilized in the study.

Qualitative research

Put simply, qualitative research is an investigation of social phenomena that is dependent on words as opposed to numbers. Unlike quantitative research, words used by participants to describe their experiences, views, conceptions, beliefs, etc. form the data that are analysed by researchers. Qualitative research requires as much rigour and soundness as quantitative research and there are ways of doing so that are specific to qualitative research. In qualitative research rigour is in terms of authenticity of data and possible transferability of findings from one context to a similar context. The equivalent of authenticity and transferability in quantitative research are reliability and validity, respectively. There are various qualitative methodological approaches, which include grounded theory approach, phenomenology and ethnography.

Grounded theory approach

The grounded theory approach is based on raw data from which themes, interpretations, or propositions can be derived. The idea is not to restrict findings to the realm of pre-existing theories or hypotheses but to let the qualitative raw data reveal possible theories or hypotheses. Although slight variations in the approach to grounded theory have emerged between the two founders of the theory, Strauss and Glaser, the fundamental aim of the theory, which is to 'explore basic social processes and to understand the multiplicity of interactions that produces variation in that process' (Heath and Cowley, 2004), remains the same. The variations are mainly to do with the way data are coded and analysed inductively, giving rise to 'Straussian' and 'Glaserian' approaches to qualitative data analysis (Heath and Cowley, 2004).

Phenomenology

The basis of a phenomenological approach is a phenomenon of interest, which in simple terms is an experience of interest. The conceptions, views, reactions, feelings of an individual or a particular group of individuals with regard to a specific phenomenon under investigation are gathered and then analysed in order to understand the phenomenon and the experiences of the people affected or involved.

Ethnography

Ethnographic research design is naturalistic observational research that is dependent on the researcher joining and becoming part of the people or culture that is being studied in order to be able to observe directly what goes on in real-life settings. Thus, qualitative data are gathered through direct observations made by the researcher over a period that is generally six months or more. Thus, there are no interviews per se, the researcher tries to blend with the people being studied as much as possible so as to be exposed to their conceptions, views, expectations, feelings, etc. regarding the topic under investigation.

Experimental research

Categories (c) and (d) require the researcher to do something that may change the outcome variable that is being measured. Thus, the researcher does not merely observe a phenomenon/problem but manipulates it in order to find out if the manipulation changes the outcome in one way or another. This type of research is called experimental research. The main characteristic of experimental research is that there is some kind of manipulation of independent variables which potentially affects the dependent (or outcome) variables.

Using the example of people presenting at a hospital with diarrhoea given above under observational research, let us assume that the researchers who conducted observational research (cross-sectional case control study) found out that patients presenting with diarrhoea were from communities that did not have access to safe drinking water and were using water from open shallow wells. The researchers also found out that stool samples from patients who presented with diarrhoea had *Vibrio cholerae*, a pathogen that is known to cause cholera. In addition, the researchers found out that the patients came from residential areas located in 36 different geographical areas and 80% of them were children under the age of 12. Hypothetically, one could develop an intervention that includes an educational component on how to minimize chances of being infected with water-borne diseases through such measures as boiling water before it is used for drinking purposes by people. The development of such an intervention could be based on relevant knowledge that is already available in literature.

To find out if the intervention works, one could implement the intervention on one group of communities over a certain period of time without implementing it on the other group of communities. One would then compare the incidence rates for the two groups. Such a study would be an experimental study because the researchers intervene by implementing a programme that has potential to affect the outcome variable. In order to minimize bias when selecting communities to be in the group that receives the intervention, called the experimental group, or the group that does not receive the intervention, the control group, the researcher has to randomly allocate the different communities to the experimental or control group. The outcome variable, also called the dependent variable, is the incidence of diarrhoea over a stipulated period of time and it is compared between the experimental and control groups. If the intervention is effective, the incidence for the experimental group should be significantly lower than that for the control group. The researcher has to find out if the difference between the incidence rates for the two groups is statistically significant.

Continuum of control in research

The level of control of variable increases from naturalistic observational research though participant observational research to experimental research. In naturalistic observational research the researcher merely observes a phenomenon without attempting to manipulate any variable. Thus, from purely naturalistic observational research to participant observational research there is a continuum of intrusion by the researcher which increases from the naturalistic to the participant observational research. Thus, there is no clear-cut division between naturalistic and participant observational research. Instead, the level of involvement of external factors gradually increases from the naturalistic to the participant observational type of research. However, the involvement of the researcher in observational research does not necessarily amount to deliberate control of certain variables; any effect is unintended because it is simply due to the mere involvement of the researcher. For example, if a researcher is observing how teachers teach in a classroom, the mere presence of the researcher may affect the behaviour of the teacher and students to some extent, even though that is not the intention of the researcher.

In contrast, in experimental research the researcher deliberately controls certain variables with the exception of the outcome variable which (the outcome variable) is then measured in one way or another. Using the simple example of observational research on the way kudus live and interact in their natural environment, researchers should not control anything in the natural environment of the kudus. On the other hand, the example of an experimental study to find out if a certain educational intervention could effectively arrest the problem of diarrheal outbreaks would necessitate control of various aspects of the research by the researchers. For instance, the researchers would deliberately allocate certain participants to a control group that does not receive the interventional programme while allocating other participants to the experimental group that would undergo the interventional program. The allocation would be done through a process of randomization to ensure that there is no bias in the process of allocating the villages to one group or the other. The researchers would also deliberately ensure that the only difference between the two groups of the participants would be the presence or absence of the intervention; everything else should be same between the two groups.

Fig. 4.2 shows the continuum of researchers' control in different research designs.

Variables

A variable is a parameter that may vary from one research participant to another. Due to the aspect of measuring, variables are a feature of quantitative research and not qualitative research. For example, if one wants to find out the extent to which obesity is a problem affecting primary school-aged children in a certain province, one needs to go and measure the height and mass of the primary school children in that province. The parameters height and mass are variables because they may be different from one child to the next one. Height and mass are used to calculate the body mass index (BMI) for each child. BMI is given by dividing the squared height by the mass. If BMI is above $25\,kg/m^2$, the child is considered to be obese. It means that the outcome variable is the BMI which is based on two variables, the height and mass. It may also be important to find out if there is any difference between biological girls and boys in terms of their BMI. In other words, one may want to find out if biological gender has a bearing on obesity. Thus, while measuring height and mass, the biological gender of each and every child is also recorded. It means that biological gender is also another variable that can be measured.

Variables can be considered to be 'tangible' if they can be physically and directly measured. In the example above, height, mass and gender could be viewed as 'tangible' variables. Positivistic research paradigm is to a large extent based on tangible variables that can be measured objectively without being affected by social factors surrounding the participants or the researchers. Thus, positivistic view is that height and mass are tangible and objective quantitative variables that have some 'true' values that are not affected by any value systems or social context. The same applies to biological gender, which can be considered to be a tangible variable. Gender in general may be socially constructed,

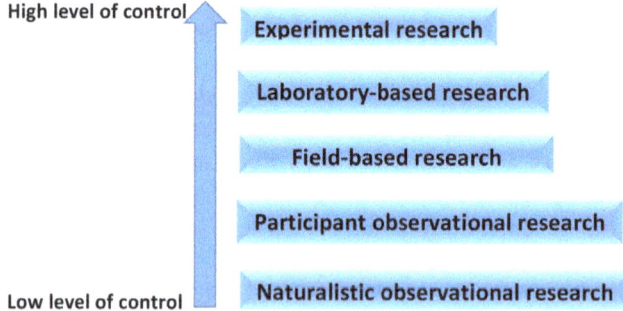

Figure 4.2 Diagram showing continuum of control by researchers in different research designs.

which would make it a subjective and 'non-tangible' variable, as some people may prefer to be of different gender to their biological gender.

If researchers also wanted to find out if the children are knowledgeable about factors that are associated with obesity they may administer a questionnaire that is designed in such a way that it can indirectly determine whether a child is knowledgeable about factors associated with obesity or not. The questionnaire would have questions aimed at eliciting answers that demonstrate knowledge about factors associated with obesity. Such knowledge about factors associated with obesity would vary from one child to another. Knowledge would be a variable which has to be measured indirectly and to some extent subjectively. The researchers have to develop an instrument (questionnaire) that measures the kind of knowledge that they are looking for and not some other knowledge. To ensure that the instrument measures what it is intended to measure, the reliability and validity of the instrument have to be ascertained.

Examples of some 'tangible' variables

- Students' marks;
- Gender;
- Salary;
- Death;
- Postgraduate throughput rate;
- Births;
- National gross domestic product;
- Height;
- Mass;
- Antibody levels;
- Price of gold per ounce;
- Number of pathogens;
- Temperature;
- Diastolic blood pressure;
- Cholesterol levels, etc.

Examples of some 'subjective' variables

- Knowledge;
- Intelligence;
- Students' satisfaction;
- Customer satisfaction;
- Attitudes;
- Disability;
- Pain;
- Quality of life, etc.

Types of variables

Variables can be classified into two main types, categorical and continuous variables. Categorical variables can be further divided into three subgroups, nominal, ordinal and geometric variables. Types of variables are referred to as scales of measurement and they are explained below.

Categorical variables

1. Nominal level data: nominal variables have categories that are mutually exclusive. For example, biological gender is a nominal variable that has two mutually exclusive categories, male or female. Each category can be labelled with a number, for example, male = 1, female = 2, but there is no hierarchal relationship between the numerical labels. In other words, it does not mean that female is higher than male. The numerical labels of the nominal categories are assigned arbitrarily. Thus, male could be labelled 7 and female 9, or the other way around.
2. Ordinal level data: ordinal variables are mutually exclusive categories like nominal variables but they have hierarchal relationship. For example, one could assess the ability of double amputees fitted with prosthetic legs to walk and use the following categories; 1 = unable to walk, 2 = able to walk with cane or 3 = able to walk without cane. Thus category 3 has a higher value than categories 2 and 1 in terms of ability to walk using prosthetic legs. If one was comparing two hospitals in terms of the outcomes of post-amputation rehabilitation of double amputees, scores for each of the 3 categories could be added and averaged for each hospital so that the overall means for the two hospitals can be compared.

Continuous variables

A continuous variable is a variable that has an infinity number of possible values between its expected minimum and maximum values. For example, if a lorry can carry a maximum of 800kg, it means that materials that can be put onto the lorry can weigh anything between zero and 800 kg. The weight could be 100.1211kg, or 745kg or 468.45kg. Other simple examples of continuous variables are height and temperature.

In other words, a continuous variable can have fractional values, i.e. values with decimal points like 33.56 or 8.5. Continuous variables can be intervals or ratios. The difference between the two is that intervals do not have true zero whereas ratios have true zero values.

1. Intervals: interval scale of measurement has equal difference between the scale points. A simple example is temperature; the difference between 2°C and 3°C is equal to the difference 7°C and 8°C. Similarly, difference between 13°C and 23°C is the same as the difference between 24°C and 34°C. Interval scale enables magnitude to be compared, e.g. 49 C is bigger (hotter) than 22°C. However, a temperature of

0°C does not mean that there is absolutely no temperature. The zero temperature could be set anywhere on the scale.
2. Ratios: ratio scales have magnitude which can be compared, intervals between units and they have an absolute zero. An example is weight which has an absolute zero. Another example of such a variable is height because it is possible to have zero height.

References

Heath, H., and Cowley, S. (2004). Developing a grounded theory approach: a comparison of Glaser and Strauss. Int. J. Nurs. Stud. *41*, 141–150.

Reliability and Validity of Quantitative Research Instruments

5

Aceme Nyika

Graduate Support, Research and Innovation Department, University of Pretoria, Pretoria, South Africa.

Correspondence: nyikaa@yahoo.com

https://doi.org/10.21775/9781910190753.05

Abstract

Quantitative research involves collection and analysis of empirical data in order to answer specific research questions. The quality of research findings depends to a large extent on the appropriateness and quality of research instruments or tools used to collect data, the way the data are analysed and the interpretation thereof. If the data collection instruments are flawed in one way or another, then the data collected and the findings of the research are also flawed. Appropriateness and quality of research instruments pertain to the reliability and validity of the instruments. This article explains the meaning and different types of reliability and validity of quantitative research instruments. Diagrams that help to make the explanations easy to understand are used

Introduction

Reliability is a term that pertains to instruments that are used in quantitative research. Instruments are any tools that are used to measure specific variables in quantitative observational or experimental research. In simple terms, reliability of an instrument is the extent to which results derived from the instrument are repeatable or reproducible. In other words, it is a measure of the consistency of an instrument. Reliability of an instrument can be determined and expressed quantitatively. There are different types of instruments for quantitative research. Consequently, there are different types of reliability which depend on the research design and the instruments used.

Validity is the extent to which an instrument measures what it is meant to measure. Although reliability of an instrument is necessary, it is not sufficient to ensure that research findings are accurate and acceptable to the wider research community. To understand the relationship and difference between reliability and validity let us consider a very simplified hypothetical example. Suppose a researcher wants to conduct a study focused on how fast people eating a certain diet gain weight over a stipulated period. Let us assume that the researcher uses a thermometer to measure temperature of the participating people and the thermometer is very reliable in the sense that if the temperature of an individual participant is measured repeatedly at a time a consistent temperature is found. However, the research question is such that temperature measurements are not relevant, even though the instrument used is very reliable. Thus, the test is not valid for the research question that has to be answered. An instrument that enables weight to be measured should be used. This article explains the different types of reliability and validity of quantitative research instruments

Types of reliability of quantitative instruments

There are different types of reliability of instruments which include test–retest reliability, internal consistency reliability, intra-rater reliability and inter-rater reliability. The type of reliability that is relevant to an instrument depends on the nature of the instrument. The different types of reliability are shown in Fig. 5.1 and are explained in the following sections.

Test–retest reliability

This type of reliability is applicable to self-reported measures. The aim is to find out the level of reliability of responses elicited from respondents by the instrument (Vézina-Im et al. 2016). In simple terms, test–retest reliability is the extent to which answers given by particular participants to questions in a self-reported questionnaire are exactly the same when the participants are asked to complete the same questionnaire for the second time. Any differences between responses given by particular respondents to the same questions first time and second time compromise test–retest reliability. To determine test–retest reliability, the correlation between the answers obtained first time around and those obtained second time around is calculated and it is given as the test–retest reliability coefficient.

There are a number of potential causes of the discrepancies between answers provided in the first round and those provided in the second round of completing the same questionnaire. One of the possible causes is ambiguity of the questions that are in the questionnaire which may lead to the respondents understanding the questions in one way first time around and understanding the same questions differently when the

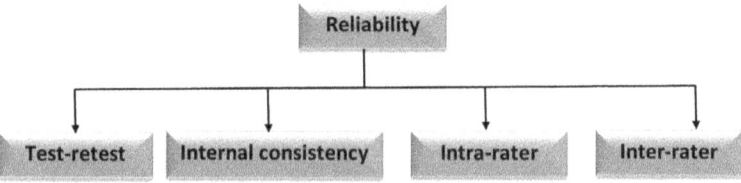

Figure 5.1 Types of reliability.

questionnaire is administered again. Another possible cause is recall error which is due to the respondents forgetting certain details of what they are being asked about.

Internal consistency reliability

The internal consistency reliability measures the consistency of the various items in an instrument in terms of eliciting information that is relevant to the constructs that are being investigated. The interconnectedness of the questions in a questionnaire has a bearing on internal consistency reliability. Thus, having some questions that are 'off-topic' compromises the internal consistency reliability of an instrument. For instance, if an instrument is meant to measure comprehension of something, including some questions that ask about emotions compromises internal consistency reliability.

Intra-rater reliability

Intra-rater reliability measures the consistency with which a single rater scores the same outcome measure (Blake *et al.*, 2016). The aim is to establish the extent to which a rater will give the same score if asked to blindly assess the same outcome more than once. For example, in a study involving quantification of microorganisms under a microscope, a rater may be given a set of 30 slides labelled 1 to 30 to estimate the number of microorganisms on each slide. Afterwards, the same slides are labelled differently (without the knowledge of the rater), for example the labels can be reversed so that what was slide 1 becomes slide 30 and vice versa. The rater is then asked to estimate the microorganism on each slide. The same process can be repeated several times so that for each slide there are several estimated numbers of microorganisms. The smaller the variation between the estimated numbers for each slide the greater the intra-rater reliability.

Inter-rater reliability

If there is more than one rater, then it is important to find out if they can rate the outcome more or less the same way (Takeuchi *et al.*, 2016). Thus, the raters can be asked to rate the same outcome and then their scores are compared to figure out the level of variation between them. There should be acceptable inter-rater reliability so that any differences that may be detected in the data collected by the different raters are genuine differences due to differences in the phenomenon being investigated instead of differences due to discrepancies in the scoring done by the different raters.

Types of validity of quantitative instruments

Validity of quantitative research instruments can be determined quantitatively. There are different types of validity which depend on the research design. The types of validity include face validity, content validity, construct validity and criterion validity. Fig. 5.2 shows the different types of validity and they are explained in detail in sections that follow.

Face validity

Face validity is the face value of an instrument which is based on the general impression that one gets when one sees the instrument. Thus, face validity is the extent to which an

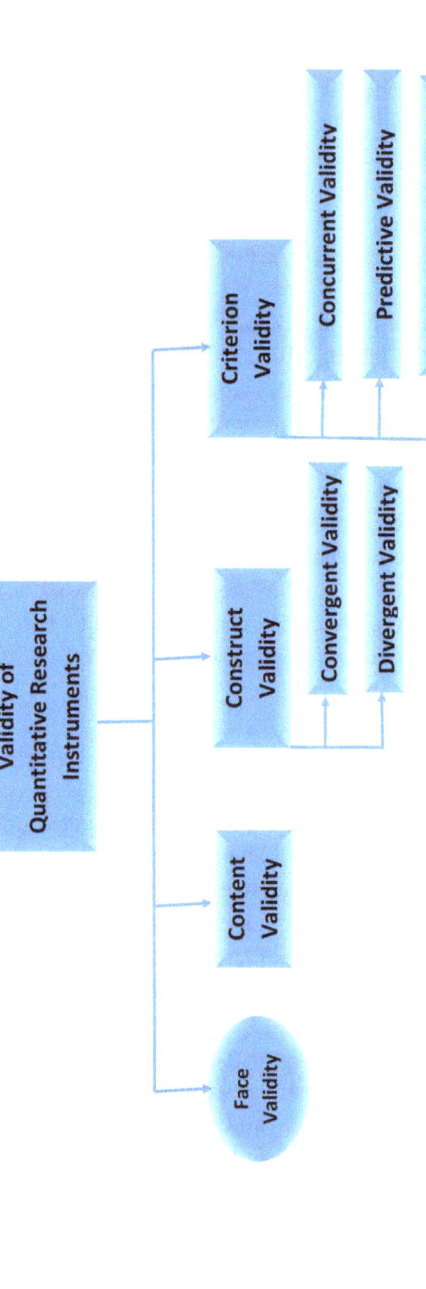

Figure 5.2 Types of validity of quantitative research instruments.

instrument appears to be capable of measuring what it is purported to measure. Unlike other types of validity which can be calculated statistically, face validity is qualitative and to a large extent subjective. The other types of validity that can be determined quantitatively are to a large extent objective.

Content validity

Content validity defines how well items in an instrument capture all aspects necessary to adequately measure the concept being investigated. Content validity is also called rational or logical validity. To explain content validity using a hypothetical example, let us suppose that an institution of higher education wants to employ a candidate capable of teaching research paradigms and methodologies at undergraduate and postgraduate levels. The institution designs a test to be used for the selection process. Applicants are then asked to write the selection test and the candidate with the highest mark is selected and offered the job. However, after a few months of teaching the institution realizes that the candidate is performing very poorly according to evaluations by students as well as peer evaluations. The teaching and learning experts then discover that 80% of the questions that were in the test used to select the candidate were about observational quantitative research and only the remaining 20% covered research paradigms and other types of research methodologies such as experimental research, qualitative research and mixed-methods research. It means therefore that the test that was used as an instrument to determine knowledge of research paradigms and methodologies had a poor content validity. It follows that content validity is a prerequisite for criterion validity because if an instrument has a low content validity it cannot have high criterion validity.

Construct validity

Construct validity defines how well a test or experiment measures up to its claims (Mciza et al., 2005; Blake et al., 2016). A test designed to measure depression must only measure that particular construct, not closely related constructs such as anxiety or stress. There are two types of construct validity: convergent and discriminant validity (Kageyama et al., 2016; Takeuchi et al., 2016). Convergent validity tests if constructs in an instrument that should be related are, in fact, related. On the other hand, discriminant validity (which is also called divergent validity) tests if constructs in an instrument that should not be related do not show any relationship.

Construct validity can be determined experimentally, and that is part of a validation process of an instrument. One way of determining construct validity is use of differential groups study which involves comparing performances of two groups; one group is tested with the instrument containing the specific construct in question and the other group is tested with the instrument without the construct in question. If there is statistically significant difference between the performances of the two groups then it means that the construct in question is important and should be part of the instrument. If the difference is not statistically significant then it means that the construct is not important and should be excluded from the instrument.

Another way of determining construct validity is called intervention study. Performance is measured using the instrument containing the construct in question and then those with poor performance are taught the construct. After teaching the construct the group is tested again using the same instrument. If the difference between the pre-intervention and post-intervention performances is statistically significant it means that the construct is important and should be part of the instrument. If the difference is not statistically significant it means that the construct is not important and should be excluded from the instrument.

There are many different ways of determining construct validity depending on the research design and the nature of the instrument. It may be possible to use a combination of various approaches to test construct validity. The different approaches will require appropriate statistical tests to be used to determine if performances of different groups or pre–post-intervention performances are statistically different. Analysis of variance (ANOVA), correlation coefficients, exploratory factor analysis, confirmatory factor analysis (Busonera *et al.*, 2016), etc. may be used. It is not possible to conduct all the possible validation tests for construct validity, hence researchers aim to provide adequate evidence to convince their peers that the instrument has sufficient construct validity for the intended purposes.

Criterion validity

This is the extent to which an instrument predicts a particular outcome measure correctly (Garton *et al.*, 2000). Statistical correlation coefficient is used to determine how close the predictions are to the actual outcome. The greater the correlation coefficient, r, the stronger is the validity of the instrument. There are three types of criterion validity depending on whether the outcome measure is in the future, is current or was in the past. The first type of criterion validity is predictive criterion validity, which pertains to an instrument that is used to predict an outcome that will occur in future. Concurrent criterion validity pertains to an instrument that is used to 'predict' an outcome measure that is occurring at the same time as the collection of prediction data are being collected. If the instrument is used to 'predict' an outcome that happened in the past, then the criterion validity that has to be considered is called postdictive criterion validity. However, postdictive criterion validity is rarely used by researchers. The three types of criterion validity are explained in detail below.

Predictive criterion validity

This validity determines if an instrument correctly predicts what it is supposed to predict. For instance, one may want to predict future performance in mathematics at secondary school through an instrument that tests some aspects of knowledge of children in primary school. The predictor instrument would be meant to determine an outcome measure, performance in secondary school-level mathematics, before it happens. The extent to which the instrument can predict correctly performance in secondary school level mathematics would be its predictive criterion validity. To determine the predictive criterion validity of the instrument, the correlation between the predicted and the actual performance in secondary school mathematics for a particular sample of students would be calculated. Another example is an instrument used to predict election results. The instrument would be used in advance of upcoming elections to predict the percentage votes for various political parties that will be contesting in the elections. After the actual election results are out, the predicted results would then be compared with the actual results to determine the predictive criterion validity of the instrument used.

Concurrent criterion validity

Concurrent validity of an instrument is measured against an existing test that may be considered to be a standard or benchmark (Mciza et al., 2005; Blake, Raker and Whelan, 2016). Suppose researchers have developed a shorter and cheaper instrument than an existing test that was validated. The higher the correlation between the scores obtained using the newly developed instrument under investigation and those obtained using the established instrument the higher the concurrent validity of the former instrument. One major limitation of concurrent criterion validity is the requirement for an existing criterion against which a newly developed criterion can be benchmarked. If there is no such existing criterion then criterion validity cannot be determined.

However, criterion validity does not necessarily have to be benchmarked against a proper instrument that already exists; a new instrument can be tested against a criterion of interest. For instance, an organization may be interested in developing an instrument that can help to determine level of performance in a data-capturing department. Firstly, the criterion for measuring performance in data capturing should be established. The criterion could include the quantity of data captured per unit time and quality of the captured data in terms of absence of errors and omissions. Secondly, an instrument that could potentially identify level of performance in capturing data should be developed based on existing theoretical knowledge, experience, findings from prior research and or expert advice. The instrument could be a test that focuses on content and constructs believed to be relevant to data capturing. After pilot testing the instrument, it could then be administered on candidates whose levels of performance in data capturing have been determined using the criterion already developed. The correlation between the outcomes of the test and the outcomes of the performance criterion is the criterion validity.

If the correlation is acceptably high, the test could be used for predictive purposes to screen applicants wanting to be employed as data capturers. Thus, it is possible to administer that test in order to select applicants to be employed. Those who get high marks are selected for employment. To determine if the test is a good predictor of levels of performance in data capturing, the levels of performance in data capturing of the employed candidates are correlated with the marks they got when they wrote the selection test in the first place. The extent to which the selection test marks correlate with the performance scores is the predictive criterion validity.

Postdictive criterion validity

If an instrument is designed to determine something that happened in the past, then the extent to which it does so accurately is the postdictive criterion validity (Lussier et al., 2011). For instance, an instrument could be developed to determine retrospectively the secondary school educational characteristics of students who pass first year university examinations with distinctions. Thus, the starting point is the first year university students and then their secondary school educational records are dug up to determine if they could have predicted the first year university performance.

Figure 5.3 Diagram illustrating the relationship between reliabilty and validity of an instrument.

Reliability and validity of quantitative instruments

It is possible to have a reliable instrument that lacks validity, but it is no,t possible for an instrument to have validity if it is not reliable. In other words, reliability is a prerequisite for validity. Thus, an instrument can reliably measure something that is not what it is meant to measure. Fig. 5.3 shows that although an instrument may reliably hit the red spot, that may not be the intended target of the research

References

Busonera, A., Cataudella, S., Lampis, J., Tommasi, M., and Zavattini, G.C. (2016). Investigating validity and reliability evidence for the maternal antenatal attachment scale in a sample of Italian women. Arch. Womens Ment. Health *19*, 329–336. https://doi.org/10.1007/s00737-015-0559-3

Garton, B., Dyer, J., and King, B. (2000), The use of learning styles and admission criteria in predicting academic performance and retention of college freshmen, Journal of Agricultural Education, *41*(2), 46–53.

Mciza, Z., Goedecke, J.H., Steyn, N.P., Charlton, K., Puoane, T., Meltzer, S., Levitt, N.S., and Lambert, E.V. (2005). Development and validation of instruments measuring body image and body weight dissatisfaction in South African mothers and their daughters. Public Health Nutr. *8*, 509–519.

Kageyama, M., Nakamura, Y., Kobayashi, S., and Yokoyama, K. (2016).Validity and reliability of the Family Empowerment Scale for caregivers of adults with mental health issues. J. Psychiatr. Ment. Health Nurs. 23, 521–531. https://doi.org/10.1111/jpm.12333

Lussier, P., Corrado, R., Healey, J., Tzoumakis, S., and Deslauriers-Varin, N. (2011). The CRACOW instrument for multi-problem violent youth: examining the postdictive validity with a sample of preschoolers. International Journal of Child, Youth and Family Studies 2(1), 294–329.

Mciza, Z., Goedecke, J.H., Steyn, N.P., Charlton, K., Puoane, T., Meltzer, S., Levitt, N.S., and Lambert, E.V. (2005). Development and validation of instruments measuring body image and body weight dissatisfaction in South African mothers and their daughters. Public Health Nutr. *8*, 509–519.

Takeuchi, H., Fervaha, G., Lee, J., Agid, O., and Remington, G. (2016). A preliminary examination of the validity and reliability of a new brief rating scale for symptom domains of psychosis: Brief Evaluation of Psychosis Symptom Domains (BE-PSD). Journal of Psychiatric Research *80*, 87–92.

Vézina-Im, L., Godin, G., Couillard, C., Perron, J., Lemieux, S., and Robitaille, J. (2016).Validity and reliability of a brief selfreported questionnaire assessing fruit and vegetable consumption among pregnant women. BMC Public Health *16*, 982. https://doi.org/10.1186/s12889-016-3656-y

Writing a Research Proposal: From Title Through Research Question and Conceptual Framework to Methodology

Aceme Nyika

Graduate Support, Research and Innovation Department, University of Pretoria, Pretoria, South Africa.

Correspondence: nyikaa@yahoo.com

https://doi.org/10.21775/9781910190753.06

Abstract

Writing a research proposal is an important step in postgraduate programmes that require research projects to be conducted. Put simply, a research proposal is a detailed plan of the research project that one wants to conduct. Thus, the proposal addresses the 'what' and 'how' questions about the intended research project. In addition, research proposals enable academic institutions to assess if their postgraduate candidates have adequate comprehension of the research process to be able to conduct research properly. Although the exact format of research proposals may vary from one subject area to another and from one academic institution to another, there are some fundamental components which are to a large extent universal. This chapter walks the reader though the process of writing a research proposal, starting from title through research question, theoretical framework and conceptual framework to research methodology.

Introduction

It is critical to have a clear and well-thought-out proposal before embarking on the actual research project because the proposal helps to give the researcher direction in terms of formulation of research question or objective, relevant literature to read, methodological approach to data collection, data analysis methods and interpretation of the analysed data in order to answer the research question. The process of developing and polishing up a proposal enhances comprehension of each important stage of the proposed research. A clear conceptualization of research at the proposal stage goes a long way in facilitating the task of writing up the findings. For instance, the introduction that is in the research proposal forms the basis of chapter 1 of a thesis, dissertation or research report. Similarly, the literature review and methods form the basis of chapters 2 and 3, respectively. All that needs to be done is to beef up what was written in the proposal and change the future tense that was used in various parts of the proposal, especially in the methods section, to past tense as, at the point of reporting findings, the research methods would have been implemented.

Research proposals for different postgraduate programmes differ in terms of depth and scope of the proposed research. For instance, a proposal for a doctorate degree programme would be to greater depth and scope than lower postgraduate programmes because doctorate research has to contribute some new knowledge to the existing body of knowledge whereas research projects for lower postgraduate programmes have to demonstrate comprehension of the research process without necessarily contributing new knowledge. Thus, a desk-top literature review project may suffice for a postgraduate diploma or honours degree programme but it would be inadequate for a doctorate degree.

The most fundamental components of research proposals are title, introduction, statement of the research problem, research question and or research hypothesis, specific objectives, literature review, research methodology, activity plan, budget and references. How the contents are structured may vary from one institution to another based on preferred formats. For instance, some institutions may want the literature review to be imbedded into the introduction instead of having it in a separate section. For some institutions proposal formats for lower postgraduate programmes such as diplomas and honours degrees may be different from formats for higher postgraduate programmes such as masters and doctorate degrees. Nevertheless, the information that should be in a proposal remains more or less the same even if it may be packed differently. Fig. 6.1 shows a template of a general structure of a research proposal and the constituent components are explained in more detail in sections that follow.

Title

A title of a research project proposal should capture the gist of the intended study. It should be concise but as comprehensive as possible. In general, a title should have around 25 words. A good title reflects the gap in knowledge that the proposed study is aimed at addressing. However, at the stage of writing a research proposal the title may be tentative because it may be amended later based on comments from supervisors and or assessors. The title may also be amended as the actual research progresses

At the proposal stage a good title is important because it predisposes readers favourably towards the proposal. If you eventually publish your research findings, a good catchy title draws attention of readers to your article and it entices them to read your work.

Introduction

The main aim of an introduction is to put your study into the context of what is already known. It gives a background upon which the proposed study is based. To give the context, an introduction should start with the 'big picture' of the subject area and it should then be narrowed down to the focus of the proposed study (Fig. 6.2). Although different

Research Proposal Template

1. Title
2. Introduction
    - 2.1 The broad picture first then the 'gap' in knowledge
    - 2.2 Statement of the problem
    - 2.3 Research question and / or hypothesis
    - 2.4 Aim or main objective of the proposed study
    - 2.5 Specific objectives of the study
3. Literature Review
    - 3.1 Critical appraisal of literature
    - 3.2 Theoretical framework
    - 3.3 Conceptual framework
4. Methodology
    - 4.1 Research design
    - 4.2 Target population and sampling technique
    - 4.3 Data collection methods and procedures
        - Type of data to be collected (e.g. variables for quantitative research, qualitative information for qualitative research, etc.)
        - Data collection methods (e.g. samples for laboratory measurements, questionnaires, interviews, archived records, etc.)
        - Pilot study (if applicable)
        - Data collection instruments: Reliability and validity issues for quantitative research or authenticity and transferability issues for qualitative research (if applicable)
    - 4.4 Data analysis and interpretation
        - Analysis methods (e.g. statistical tests, laboratory analyses, qualitative analyses, etc. for quantitative research; coding, thematic analysis, content analysis, etc. for qualitative research)
        - Interpretation criteria (e.g. levels of significance, confidence intervals, statistical power, etc. for quantitative research
5. Ethical Issues
    - Ethical principles
    - Informed consent (if applicable)
    - Privacy and confidentiality issues
    - Approvals (ethical, institutional, community, etc.)
6. Budget
7. Activity plan
8. References
9. Appendices (if applicable)

Figure 6.1 Template of a general structure of a research proposal.

academic institutions may have different requirements, in general an introduction should contain background, statement of the problem, research question(s), main objective or hypothesis and specific objectives. It may not be possible to have all these components

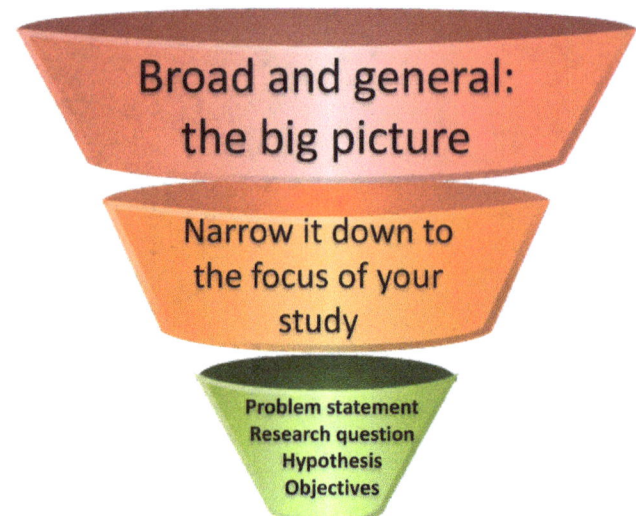

Figure 6.2 General structure of introduction section.

depending on the nature of research being proposed. For instance, exploratory observational research may not have research hypotheses *a priori*; hence research question(s) and objectives may suffice. Some institutions require statement of the problem, main objective and specific objectives to be stated without explicitly stating research questions.

Statement of the problem

Statement of the problem is the gap in knowledge that the researcher wants to address. The gap should be made conspicuous to the reader by giving a clear background in terms of what is already known and what is still outstanding. Although the statement of the problem has to be stated explicitly, the whole introductory section should coherently but implicitly build up to the statement.

Research question and or hypothesis

Expressing the focus of a research project as a research question helps to guide the whole research process from the proposal writing stage through data collection and analysis to formulating a conclusion that is rooted in the analysed data. For some research projects there may be a main research question and some secondary research questions. The main research question is to a large extent derived from the statement of the problem, which in turn is rooted in the title of the research project. The research question gives a hint to the reader in terms of the research design to be used and variables to be measured.

Research hypothesis

A research hypothesis is an a priori proposition put forward to explain a phenomenon under investigation. Based on what is already known in the subject area, the researcher makes a reasonable 'guess' as to what the answer to the research question could be. This is possible if the research is being done from a positivistic point of view which postulates that there is absolute reality which researchers strive to uncover. For this type of research, data analysis and interpretations are done deductively, the aim being to prove or disprove the set research hypothesis.

For some research projects, the main research hypothesis can be stated as the null and alternative hypotheses. The null hypothesis is the position that any difference that is observed (through analysis of the collected data) between aspects of the phenomenon being investigated is due to chance and is thus not statistically significant. The alternative hypothesis states that the difference observed is statistically significant, which means that there is a real difference between the aspects being investigated.

Aim or main objective of the study

The aim of a study is more or less the same as the main objective of the study. It succinctly informs the reader the gist of the study and is closely linked to the research question and/or hypothesis. It tells the reader what the study is intended to address. The aim or main objective has a verb that is key to the methodology that has to be used. For instance, if the aim of a study is to compare the quantity and quality of postgraduate students produced by universities within a particular country, it means that the study will involve assessing the numbers of university postgraduate students and their quality. The term quality will have to be defined and should be based on proven evidence or theories. The way the quality will be assessed should be based on empirical evidence so that there is certainty that it will indeed measure quality of postgraduate students.

Specific objectives

Specific objectives could be considered to be the steps that need to be taken in order to achieve the main objective of the study. In other words, the main objective has to be broken down into specific objectives that explicitly state what exactly should be done. The specific objective should be SMART.

- **S**pecific: focusing on one issue.
- **M**easurable: should be a clear issue that can be assessed.
- **A**ttainable: should be feasible in terms of available resources and expertise.
- **R**elevant: should be related to the research question.
- **T**ime-bound: should be accomplishable within the time frame for the research project.

In order to clarify what exactly should be done, specific objectives are centred on verbs. Phrasing specific objectives as 'to measure', 'to compare', 'to develop', 'to evaluate', etc., indicates the type of research methods that would be used. Specific objectives should form the basis of the research methodology section. For each specific objective there should be a corresponding section under methods which explains how the specific objective will be achieved. The specific objectives could also guide the development of a budget for the project. For each specific objective, the various activities that have to be performed should be budgeted for. Specific objectives can also form the basis of the activity plan.

Literature review

Literature review explains the existing knowledge that firstly forms the basis of your study and secondly shapes the way your study is to be done. In other words, the literature review forms a framework within which your research project is to be conducted. It explains further the gap in knowledge that is put forward in the introductory section and outlines the theoretical and conceptual frameworks that inform the methodological and analytical approaches to be used. For masters by research project and doctorate degree programmes it is advisable for the literature review to end with theoretical framework and conceptual frameworks for the proposed study. However, some academic institutions do not require the frameworks to be included explicitly but they should be implicitly captured in the literature review.

Critical appraisal of literature

Types of literature review

Although the term 'literature review' tends to be used to refer to any type of literature review, there are distinct types of literature review each with specific methodological approach. The different types of literature review are narrative literature review, systematic literature review, meta-analysis and meta-synthesis (Tranfield *et al.*, 2003; Cronin *et al.*, 2008; Paterson *et al.*, 2009). Some researchers have introduced another type of literature review which has been referred to as 'integrative literature review' (Torraco, 2005; Yorks, 2008; Callahan, 2010).

Narrative literature review

The most common type of literature review that is used by researchers when they publish their findings is the narrative literature review. This type involves a logical selection of a body of literature relevant to a specific subject area which is then summarized and critiqued in order to motivate for the new research that is being done on the same subject area. However, such literature review can also be done for non-research purposes such as to synthesize existing knowledge on a particular topic, to understand trends in a particular subject area or to evaluate existing knowledge and practices for the development or updating guidelines of policies.

Integrative literature review

Integrated literature review is a more thorough review than the narrative literature review but less thorough than a systematic literature review explained in the next section. It involves a clearly defined search and selection methodology and the selected literature should be analysed critically. The selected articles should be analysed individually as well as in groups of related articles. The relationship between articles could be based on methodologies used in the articles, target populations, sampling techniques used, sample sizes, settings, etc. Analysis could involve comparisons, identification of themes (common across many articles or unique to specific articles) and identification of gaps. One of the advantages of integrative literature review is that it enables analysis of articles emanating from diverse methodologies, including experimental and non-experimental methodologies (Kanfl, 2005). In general, integrative literature review has five broad stages (Kanfl, 2005). The first one is problem identification stage which is aimed at clearly identifying and defining the problem to be addressed by the review. The second one is the literature search stage which is focused on comprehensive search strategies so as to get as many critical and relevant articles as possible. The third stage is the evaluation stage which involves evaluating the articles obtained using defined criteria such as methodology, sample size, etc. The fourth stage is the data analysis stage which is focused on analysing data from the selected articles. The fifth and final stage is the presentation of the findings, which may be in the form of a model or theory proposition.

Systematic literature review
Systematic literature review is more rigorous and comprehensive than the narrative literature review. It has to have a clear research question and a clear methodology to be followed in order to answer the research question. Khan et al (2003, p. 118) posited five steps of conducting a systematic literature review, which are (i) 'framing questions for a review', (ii) 'identifying relevant work', (iii) 'assessing the quality of studies', (iv) 'summarizing the evidence' and (v) 'interpreting the findings'. Although the steps may seem to be chronological, in practice the process is iterative and some steps may be done concurrently and repeatedly. The steps show that systematic literature review is a research project in its own right, with a research question, a methodology that includes analysis and a conclusion that answers the research question. This is in spite of the fact that the literature review may be part of an overarching research project.

The starting point is the development of a research question or research questions to be answered by the systematic literature review. The identification of relevant literature involves searching for literature and screening out irrelevant materials using inclusion and exclusion criteria that form part of the methodology. When searching, words from the research question form the basis of the search-strings (also called keywords) that can be used, and the search-strings may have to be revisited several times depending on the literature that is being found.

Assessing the quality of literature found and summarizing it necessitates reading, comprehending and recording the main points or arguments. It means that the literature dug out has to be unpacked in terms of research questions that were being addressed by the authors of the published papers, research designs, target populations, sampling techniques, data collection and analysis methods and interpretation of results as reported in the published papers. Depending on the nature of the question being addressed by the systematic literature review, meta-analysis (for quantitative studies) or meta-synthesis (for qualitative studies) may be part of the overarching analysis and interpretation done in systematic literature review. It is relatively rare to have questions that require systematic reviews of both quantitative and qualitative literature; hence meta-analysis and meta-synthesis are rarely used together in systematic literature reviews.

Meta-analysis
Meta-analysis could be considered to be a form of systematic literature review aimed at answering a well-focused question through statistical analysis of a body of quantitative

studies. Quantitative findings from published studies are pooled together and then analysed using standardized statistical methods on the basis of an overall sample size derived from the pooled samples of the different studies. Meta-analysis of published research findings has been done in various areas of specialization which include clinical trials (DerSimonian and Laird, 1986), medical field (Higgins and Thompson, 2002) and observational studies (Stroup *et al.*, 2000).

Meta-synthesis
Whereas meta-analysis is based on 'pooled' quantitative studies, meta-synthesis is based on qualitative studies that are focused on a particular topic. Qualitative studies that are based on grounded theory, phenomenological or ethnographic methodologies may be integrated and analysed jointly. The aim is to synthesize new conceptualizations and or theories which may not have been synthesized on the basis of the individual studies separately. In addition, meta-synthesis can lead to the development of meta-theories that cut across several theoretical domains (Toracco, 2005).

Fundamental steps common to all types of literature review

There is no mathematical formula of doing a literature review. Different people may use different approaches and still do good literature reviews. However, there are certain fundamental tasks that should be done in a literature review regardless of the type of the literature review. The tasks include (i) searching for relevant literature, (ii) selecting and organizing literature that has to be read in detail and (iii) synthesizing the literature into a coherent appraisal in the context of your research question. These tasks are explained in detail in the sections below. The two main factors that affect literature search are the keywords used to do the search and the bibliographic databases searched. If inappropriate keywords are used then the best literature is likely to be missed. Similarly, if an inappropriate search engine is used the best literature is likely to be missed even if correct keywords may have been used.

Searching for relevant literature and choice of search words
Searching and finding the most relevant literature is the first step that can negatively affect the rest of the subsequent steps if it is not done effectively. There is so much literature available in the public domain that it can be a daunting and confusing task to search for relevant literature that one should read and critique. Thus, one has to be able to fine-tune the process of searching for literature so that it yields the most relevant articles.

The starting point could be to derive appropriate keywords on the problem, challenge, or gap that one may have identified for one's research project. This is better than using the broad subject area because there could be thousands or even millions of articles available. The title of the research project could be a good starting point in terms of words that could be used when searching for literature. Different wording can lead to different articles hence it is important to use as many different wordings as possible. It is also critical to indicate the years of interest so as to get the most recent publications. Thus, one may search for articles published in the current year and then search backwards in order to pick up literature that was published in the last five to ten years. The keywords can be amended or used in different combinations in order to increase chances of picking up the most relevant literature. The same keywords used for searching can yield different search results depending on such techniques as use of 'wildcards' and Boolean operators. An example of a wildcard is the asterisk (*) which enables different variants of literature on the same search terms to be pulled up/retrieved. Examples of Boolean operators are such words as 'or', 'and', 'not' and 'with'.

It is always important to get the most recent publications so as to be sure that what may seem to be a gap in knowledge was not addressed by other researchers recently. References that are cited in the preliminary articles that one reads are also a good pointer towards additional literature that may be relevant and useful. Some journals also list references of articles that cited a particular paper, and some of those articles may be very recent as they must have been published after the particular paper. However, searching for relevant and best literature should be a process that gets better as one gets some articles and reads them so as to figure out how best to proceed with the literature review.

Search engines and databases

It is critical to use the most appropriate search engines and to search the most relevant databases. There are databases of literature that are specific for certain fields of specialization. For instance, PubMed and Medline are generally appropriate for health-related literature whereas Google Scholar tends to cut across different fields of specialization. Some fields of specialization have their own specific databases of literature and it is a good approach to target them if they exist.

There are many databases that can be searched; some are good for specific subject areas whereas some cut across different subject areas. For instance, PsycINFO is a database for psychological literature, MathSciNet for mathematical literature (Neuhaus and Daniel, 2008) while PubMed and the Medical Literature Analysis and Retrieval System Online (Medline) are good for publications in the health-related areas. In contrast, Scopus is a multidisciplinary database of peer-reviewed literature. Another example of multidisciplinary database is the Web of Science (WoS) which is provided by Thomson Reuters (Gasparyan *et al.*, 2013). In terms of search engines, there are several that can be used but Google Scholar, which is a free multidisciplinary web-based search engine, seems to be one of the most popular and user-friendly ones (Walters, 2007; Neuhaus *et al.*, 2008; Gasparyan *et al.*, 2013).

Selecting and organizing literature that has to be read in detail

Literature search may result in so many articles that seem to be relevant that reading all of them would be almost impossible. Thus, it is necessary to screen articles and prioritize those that seem to be the most relevant. One way of screening is to read the abstract of each and every article and select those that are the most relevant to the proposed study. It is also important to organize them into groups based on concepts, themes, methodologies or any other criteria that is logical in the context of your research question. For instance, one broad categorization could be quantitative and qualitative methodologies. Within each broad category, there could be further categorisations. Articles that are more or less in agreement in terms of their findings group be grouped together. It is possible for an article to be in more than one category depending on what the focus is. For instance, an article focusing on children under the age of 5 years that is based on randomized sampling technique could be in a category for randomized studies as well as in a category of studies that focused on children.

Synthesising literature into a coherent appraisal: the five Cs
The other common features of a good literature review are generally referred to as the 'five Cs'. However, there are two versions of the five Cs. One version posits that the five Cs are concise, clear, critical, convincing, and contributive (Callahan, 2014). The other version posits that the five Cs are cite, compare, contrast, critique and connect (Mike and Steve, 2011). I think that the two versions are complementary; one describes the qualities of a good literature review and the other states what needs to be done to achieve the good qualities. In other words, for a literature review to be concise, critical, convincing and contributive, the writer should cite, compare, contrast, critique and connect what is in literature.

Citing
Citing means acknowledging the sources of factual information or arguments used in critiquing literature. For one to cite certain references one needs to do a literature search, choose relevant literature to read, read the selected literature and then cite it in the current literature review. Due to the advent of internet, there are thousands of reading materials that are accessible to readers. It means therefore that choosing what material to read and critique can be a mammoth and confusing task if it is not done logically and systematically. Unfortunately there is no mathematical formula that can be used for searching relevant literature. There are various ways that can be used and sometimes combining the different approaches can enhance the effectiveness of the literature search.

Comparing and contrasting
As one reads the relevant literature selected, it is important to compare various schools of thought on the particular matter being focused on. Thus, grouping together articles that are in agreement and then comparing them with those that have a different position helps to compare and contrast the existing schools of thought or theories. The comparing and contrasting should go beyond the conclusions of the articles and unpack the research questions, target populations, sampling techniques, sample sizes and methodological approaches used. Any limitations of the studies that could have had a bearing on the findings should also be discussed.

Critiquing and connecting
A literature review is not meant to be a mere compilation of various studies that have been conducted in the subject area of the proposed study. Citing, comparing and contrasting alone are not adequate to make a literature review concise, clear, critical, convincing, and contributive. Instead, it should be a continuation of the motivation for conducting the proposed study and justification for the methodological approach chosen. Thus, it should be part of the complex argument for conducting the proposed study. Findings reported in literature form the premises for the arguments put forward to explain the gap in knowledge and to explain the theories or concepts that shape the methodological approach to

be used in the proposed study. By so doing the researcher connects the literature review with the intended study.

To critique literature one needs to firstly comprehend the different points of view posited by different researchers. Thus, one should be able to figure out those that are in agreement or disagreement on a particular issue. It does not necessarily have to be disagreements or agreements; it could be similarities and differences in findings and or interpretations. In order for the 'voice' of the one critiquing the literature to be heard, one has to figure out what could have led to the similarities or differences. It could be due to differences in the targeted populations. It could be due to different settings that may have a bearing on the outcome variables. It could be due to differences in methodological approaches.

For instance, an observational quantitative research design may have been used in one study while in another study on the same topic an observational qualitative research design may have been used. It would therefore mean that different sampling techniques, data collection procedures, data analysis methods and interpretations would have been used. However, merely pointing out differences or similarities is not critiquing literature; the relevance to the proposed study must be explicitly articulated. In other words, there must be an argument that is being made which uses the facts from literature as premises. Thus, when one is critiquing literature, one should always be guided by the following questions:

- What point or argument do I want to make?
- What are the premises for the point/argument?
- Are the premises logically linked/related to my point/argument?
- Can the premises be verified through the references that I have provided?

Evaluating findings reported in literature should therefore entail an evaluation of the methodology used to collect data and the analysis and interpretation of results thereof. Such evaluation should include scrutiny of issues of reliability and validity of the instruments used if applicable.

Training by librarians
Most university libraries offer training on how to search for literature. It is important for postgraduate students to take advantage of such support programmes and ensure that they undergo relevant training in the early stages of the postgraduate programmes. Flawed and ineffective literature search compromises the quality of the literature review as it can only be as good as the literature that was reviewed. Thus, if very critical literature is missed, then the literature review may miss some critical findings or points that are already in the public domain. Similarly, if some most recent publications are missed, the research may pursue something that was tackled recently by other researchers.

Librarians would be able to guide postgraduate students to do subject area-specific searches which may be better and more effective than doing wide literature searches. Most university libraries also have 'libguides' which are available online and give guidelines on many issues that are pertinent to research, teaching and learning.

Theoretical framework

In order to understand and be able to write a theoretical framework, one needs know firstly its purpose and secondly how to develop it. In a nutshell, a theoretical framework defines boundaries for the intended study and gives the study a particular direction. A theoretical framework is developed by presenting relevant existing theories that are known and have been accepted in the academic world as being valid. The relevance of the theories to the research question being addressed should be explained and supported with convincing research findings reported by other researchers. A theoretical framework can be made up of one theory or several relevant theories depending on the research question and specific objectives of the proposed study. If several theories are relevant and are to be included in the framework, a critical appraisal is needed to explain how they relate to each other. Thus, relevant theories should not simply be compiled but should be unpacked in terms of how they relate to each other and to the research question at hand.

Developing a theoretical framework may begin with defining any pertinent terms. If there are different types of definitions for a particular term then they must be explained first before indicating which one will be used in the proposed study. A logical motivation for the choice of definition should be given. Thereafter, the theories and their relevance to the proposed study should be explained thoroughly. Any similarities and differences between your proposed study and other reported studies done in the same field should be analysed logically, commenting on theories used in those earlier studies. However, there are no hard and fast rules stipulating how a theoretical framework should be structured. What is critical is that it should be centred on the research question and should be coherent and logical.

Conceptual framework

A conceptual framework should be based on the theoretical framework and it should bring forth the main concepts that will be used in the proposed study. The concepts are shaped by the theoretical framework as definitions and theories articulated in the framework have a bearing on the concepts to be used. In turn, the concepts determine the type of variables that will have to be measured, the target population, the sampling technique, data collection procedures and data analysis methods. In other words, the conceptual framework underpins the methodology for the proposed study.

For quantitative research, a conceptual framework can be developed upfront based on a positivist research paradigm that is centred on collection of quantitative data to prove or disprove a certain reality or truth (research hypothesis) that is developed in advance of doing the research, is not dependent on the social context and is not value laden. This is deductive approach to research. Qualitative research paradigm involves interpretivism and constructivism based on the philosophical world view that there are different forms of reality and truth which are shaped by context. In other words, knowledge is considered to be constructed and interpreted by the players involved. Consequently, conceptual framework can be developed inductively as empirical qualitative data are gathered and analysed.

Research methodology
For soundness of the proposed study to be evaluated, details that cover the research design, target population, sampling technique, data collection procedures and data analysis methods should be included under research methodology. It is critical for this section to answer the question 'How will data be collected and analysed in order to answer the research question(s)?' It means that the research question gives direction in terms of how data should be collected and analysed.

Research design
The research design should be stated explicitly. This could be done by firstly stating whether it will be experimental or observational research and then explaining further the specific research design that will be used. The design should be explained as much as possible, covering such information as whether or not it will be quantitative, qualitative, longitudinal, cross-sectional, retrospective, prospective, etc.

Target population, sampling technique and sample size
Target population is the overall group of particular people, animals, objects or any things that the research question is about. For instance, if one wants to find out the average salary of mathematics teachers who have undergraduate degrees in mathematics as their highest academic qualification and have been employed for 5 years or less in private secondary schools in a particular country, then the population for the study are all secondary school teachers who (i) have undergraduate degrees in mathematics as their highest academic qualification, (ii) are teaching mathematics at private secondary schools in country x and (iii) have been employed as mathematics teachers for 5 years or less.

Depending on the numbers of private schools and the size of the population, it may not be possible to include the whole population in the study. The size of a population is designated N. It means that a certain number of eligible teachers has to be selected from the population. Such a selected representative group is called a sample, and its size is designated n to differentiate it from the population size.

Fig. 6.3 shows different sampling techniques that can be used for different research designs. The way the selection is done is the sampling technique which gives different types of samples. The sampling technique depends on the research question to be answered. The two broad types of sampling techniques are probability and non-probability sampling techniques. The main characteristic of probability sampling techniques is that they minimize bias in the selection process; in other words they reduce sampling bias. Consequently, randomly selected samples yield results that to a large extent can be generalized to the target population provided a minimum sample size that is adequately representative of the population has been used. In contrast, non-probability sampling is not based on a statistically calculated sample size and is not meant to lead to findings that are generalizable to the target population. Thus, non-probability sampling techniques yield findings which are context specific and may not be generalized to the target population.

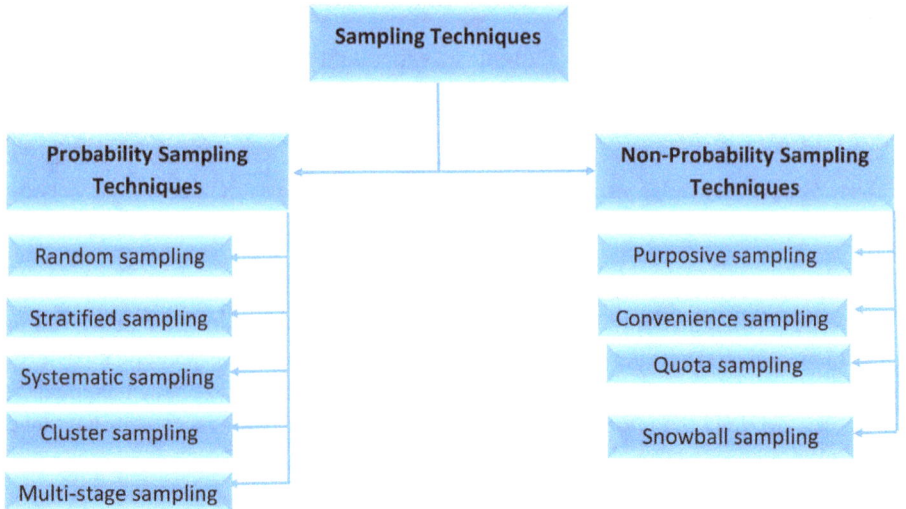

Figure 6.3 Sampling techniques.

Probability sampling techniques are commonly used for quantitative research designs while non-probability sampling techniques are generally used for qualitative research designs.

Random sampling is aimed at ensuring that each and every member of the target population has an equal chance of being selected into the sample. In other words, the aim is to minimize sampling error. The simplest way of randomly selecting a sample would be to use a coin after having decided which outcome between head and tail should mean being selected into the sample. However, this rather rudimentary way of randomization may not be practically possible due to various reasons. Consequently, computer-generated random numbers are used to randomly select a sample from a population.

Stratified random sampling is appropriate if the target population is heterogeneous and can be divided into different categories, called strata, which are intrinsically homogeneous. Random sampling technique would then be used within each stratum. The size of the sample from each stratum would depend on the weight of the particular stratum in relation to the overall target population. If the total number of population units in stratum f is Nf and the size of the overall target population is N, then the weight of stratum f is $Wf = Nf/N$.

Systematic sampling uses an ordered approach that selects study participants on the basis of specific intervals determined by the researchers upfront. Thus, the first participant is selected randomly from the target population, and then every nth candidate is selected. Systematic sampling technique is suitable for homogenous populations that can be ordered. A simple example to illustrate how systematic sampling is done is a case of a researcher wanting to find out the views of patients who attend a certain hospital. The first step would be to have a look at the average numbers of outpatients who visit the hospital per day. Depending on the general average per day, every nth outpatient is invited to participate in the study. In general, n would be more or less proportional to the daily average number of outpatients. In other words, if the general average number per day is small, then n would be proportionally small.

Cluster sampling technique is used if there are heterogeneous groups within the target population. The groups, called clusters, may be homogeneous internally. The main difference between stratified and cluster sampling techniques is that the units of analysis in cluster sampling are the clusters and not individual members of the cluster whereas in stratified sampling the units of analysis are the individual members in each stratum.

Multistage sampling technique involves randomly selecting small samples from the target population at different stages until the minimum overall sample size required has been obtained. The different stages do not constitute strata because they are to do with the timing of the sampling and they are not based on internal homogeneity as is the case with strata. Thus, the small samples randomly selected at different stages may be homogeneous or heterogeneous internally.

Purposive sampling technique involves deliberately focusing on particular members of the population whose characteristics make them the most suitable source of data to answer a particular research question. This type of sampling is usually used in qualitative studies. For instance, if one wants to conduct a study on views of policy makers on the quality of higher education in a particular country then the researcher would purposely target policy makers in the country. As there may not be many policy makers in the educational sector of a country, the researcher may invite all of the policy makers to participate in the study.

Convenient sampling technique is another sampling technique which is usually used in qualitative research. The technique is based mainly on feasibility and convenience. For instance, a study pertaining to pregnant women may make use of particular antenatal clinics because that is where it is relatively feasible and convenient to find pregnant women who may agree to participate in the study.

Data collection methods and procedures

Details of how data will be collected from the sample have to be given. If there are data collection instruments that will be used, they should be explained. Such instruments as questionnaires have to be included in the proposal as appendices. Issues of reliability and validity of the instruments have to be addressed thoroughly. If the instruments were validated previously by other researchers then details of their reliability and validity should be given. Validation of a newly developed instrument entails extensive research work that could constitute a standalone doctorate degree research project. Thus, if the aim of a study is not to validate an instrument, then appropriate ones that were already validated should be considered for use. Therefore, validation of research instruments may be beyond the scope of such postgraduate programmes as postgraduate diplomas, honours degrees and master's degrees.

Data analysis and interpretation

Analysis methods should be specified upfront before data are collected. This is a requirement for quantitative and qualitative data. The analysis should be aligned with the specific objectives so that there is more or less a corresponding data analysis for each and every specific objective. Linking the analysis to specific objectives simplifies interpretation of the results because it is clear which specific objective is being addressed by each analysis. For quantitative data any descriptive and inferential statistical analysis should be explicitly stated. For example, descriptive statistics could include means, standard deviations, ranges, interquartile ranges, demographics, etc.

In the case of inferential statistics it is important to explain the statistical tests that will be used and levels of significance. For example, if one of the specific objectives of a study is to compare performance of two athletics groups in terms of time they complete 800m race, the mean completion time for each group would be calculated. To find out if there is a statistically significant difference between the two means, a two-group t-test would be used at 5% level of significance. In some cases, a series of statistical tests have to be done depending on the outcome of some pertinent preliminary tests. For example, if a study is aimed at developing and validating a structured quantitative tool for measuring something, exploratory factor analysis would have to be done first and depending on the results of the exploratory factor analysis, confirmatory factor analysis would then be done.

Ethical issues

Before any research proposal can be implemented, it has to undergo ethical review to ensure that it does not violate the rights of people or animals. Research should also not endanger the environment. There are human ethics committees that review research proposals that affect humans. The research could be social research or it could be biomedical research. For research that involves animals, animal ethics committees review and approve the research proposals before the research can be conducted.

For research involving humans, there are four fundamental ethical principles that are used. These are the principles of autonomy, beneficence, non-maleficence and justice. Most human ethics committees use the ethical principles to weigh the potential benefits of proposed research against potential risks. The main aim of human ethics committees should be to protect the welfare of people recruited into studies.

The principle of autonomy stipulates that individual human beings have a right to self-determination; hence they should give their informed consent to voluntarily take part in any research that involves humans. To be able to give valid informed consent, firstly one should be above the legal age of majority as stipulated by national laws. If prospective research participants are minors (i.e. below the legal age of majority), their parents or legal guardians give proxy consent on their behalf. However, if the minors are old enough to comprehend what the intended research is all about, they should be asked whether or not they want to take part in the research. If they agree, they give what is called 'assent' which should still be accompanied by proxy consent. Secondly, one should be competent enough to process information and make informed decisions. Thus, if an adult is mentally ill, competence to process information and make rational informed decisions is compromised.

The principle of beneficence is about potential benefits that could be derived from the proposed research. The potential benefits should not be in the form of some undue inducement which could make the participants undergo some serious risks which they would not ordinarily be willing to undergo. Research participants should not incur any costs such as transport costs by participating in research. Thus, compensation for such costs as transport and refreshment costs should not be regarded as benefits. Benefits should be related to the actual research activities or the outcomes thereof. For instance, research participants may gain some knowledge through their participation in a research project. In some studies, like clinical trials that test medical products such as medicines and vaccines, participants may benefit from the investigational product if it turns out to be effective.

The principle of beneficence and that of non-maleficence could be considered to be two sides of the same coin. While the principle of beneficence stipulates that research should be aimed at doing good, the principle of non-maleficence stipulates that research should not cause harm to participants. The harm that could be caused may be physical, psychological or socio-economic.

The principle of justice stipulates that the recruitment of participants into research should be done fairly. In other words, there should be no bias in the selection process. The principle of justice could also be considered to be related to that of beneficence in that justice means that people who take the risk of participating in research should benefit from the outcomes of the research; it is unjust for people to carry the burden of participating in research for the benefit of others who did not carry the burden.

In order to protect the welfare of research participants, research that involves collection or use of data from human beings should be reviewed and approved by an authorized ethics committee before the research proposal can be implemented. In some cases, approvals have to be obtained from other stakeholders involved. For instance, it may be necessary to get approval from institutions, organizations, companies, etc., where data will be collected. If the proposed study involves or potentially affects certain communities, it may be necessary to consult and engage the relevant communities and get their agreement for the proposed study to be conducted. Similarly, research that make use of animals should be approved by an authorized animal ethics committee before the research can be started.

After the research proposal has been approved and the research project has started, it is important for researchers to ensure privacy and confidentiality of research participants. Information about research participants should be kept safe and secure all the time and should be accessible only to authorized research team members.

Budget

An appropriate budget should be included in a research proposal. It is important for adequate funds for a study to be secured before the study is commenced, otherwise it would be a waste of resources and time if funds were to run out before the completion of the study. One way of developing a budget is to determine the activities, equipment and or any other needs for each and every specific objective of the proposed study. After the budget, there should be a section that focuses on justification of each and every line item of the budget.

Activity plan

It is important to determine the time that will be required to do the proposed research project. An activity plan indicates the sequence in which various activities will be carried out and the estimated time each one will take to complete. It is advisable not to use dates in the activity plan because if the planned activities do not start on the estimated dates specified in the activity plan then the whole plan has to be amended. Depending on the expected duration of the whole project, weeks, months or quarters of a year etc. can be used instead of exact dates. Fig. 6.4 shows an example of a simple activity plan.

References

A proposal should be a logical motivation for doing a particular study; hence, it should be supported with empirical evidence whenever factual statements or arguments are made. Thus, references for what is already known should be provided. It is also critical to provide justification for the methodology chosen, and citing studies that successfully used the methodology before strengthens such justification.

There are various referencing styles which include Vancouver, Harvard, etc. Some academic institutions stipulate the referencing style that should be used by students. If there is no stipulated referencing style, any style can be used provided there is consistence throughout the proposal. Managing references can be simplified by use of reference management software. Some reference management programs, such as Mendeley and Zotero, are freely available.

Appendices (if applicable)

Some relevant documents may not be included in the main body of the proposal but may be included as appendices. Examples of such documents include questionnaires that will be used to collect data, a map showing the location of data collection sites, etc. It is

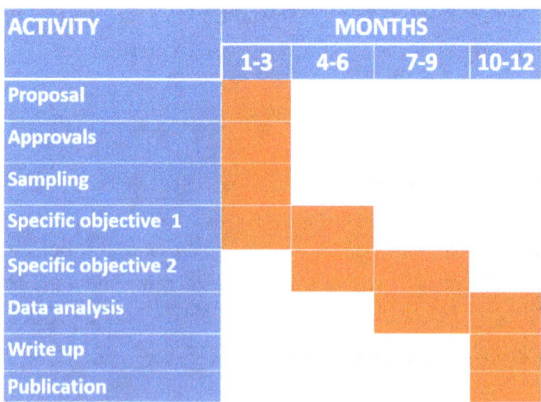

Figure 6.4 Example of a simple activity plan.

possible not to have any appendices at all; it depends on the nature of the research being proposed.

References

Callahan, J.L. (2010). Constructing a manuscript: Distinguishing integrative literature reviews and conceptual and theory articles. Human Resource Development Review 9(3), 300–304.

Callahan, J.L. (2014). Writing Literature Reviews A Reprise and Update. Human Resource Development Review. Available at: http://journals.sagepub.com/doi/full/10.1177/1534484314536705 (accessed 24 August 2017).

Cronin, P., Ryan, F., and Coughlan, M. (2008). Undertaking a literature review: a step-by-step approach. Br. J. Nurs. 17, 38–43. https://doi.org/10.12968/bjon.2008.17.1.28059

DerSimonian, R., and Laird, N. (1986). Meta-analysis in clinical trials. Control Clin Trials 7, 177–188.

Edith Cowan University. Literature review: academic tip sheet. Available at: https://intranet.ecu.edu.au/__data/assets/pdf_file/0011/20621/literature_review.pdf (accessed 7 October 2016).

Gasparyan, A.Y., Ayvazyan, L., and Kitas, G.D. (2013). Multidisciplinary bibliographic databases. J. Kor. Med. Sci. 28, 1270–1275.

Higgins, J.P., and Thompson, S.G. (2002). Quantifying heterogeneity in a meta-analysis. Stat. Med. 21, 1539–1558. https://doi.org/10.1002/sim.1186

Khan, K.S., Kunz, R., Kleijnen, J., and Antes, G. (2003). Five steps to conducting a systematic review. J. R. Soc. Med. 96, 118–121.

Mike and Steve. (2011). Doing a literature review. Available at: http://research.beccarose.co.uk/wp-content/uploads/2016/01/litReview_mike_steve_v3.pdf (accessed 7 October 2016).

Neuhaus, C., and Daniel, H.D. (2008). Data sources for performing citation analysis: an overview. J. Document. 64, 193–210.

Neuhaus, C., Neuhaus, E., and Asher, A. (2008). Google Scholar goes to school: the presence of Google Scholar on college and university Web sites. The Journal of Academic Librarianship 34(1), 39–51.

Paterson, B.L., Dubouloz, C.J., Chevrier, J., Ashe, B., King, J., and Moldoveanu, M. (2009). Conducting qualitative metasynthesis research: Insights from a metasynthesis project. Int. J. Qualit. Methods 8(3), 22–33.

Stroup, D.F., Berlin, J.A., Morton, S.C., Olkin, I., Williamson, G.D., Rennie, D., Moher, D., Becker, B.J., Sipe, T.A., and Thacker, S.B. (2000). Meta-analysis of observational studies in epidemiology: a proposal for reporting. JAMA 283, 2008–2012.

Torraco, R.J. (2005). Writing integrative literature reviews: guidelines and examples. Hum. Resource Dev. Rev. 4, 356–367.

Tranfield, D., Denyer, D., and Smart, P. (2003). Towards a methodology for developing evidence-informed management knowledge by means of systematic review. British Journal of Management 14, 207–222.

Walters, W.H. (2007). Google Scholar coverage of a multidisciplinary field. Information Processing & Management, 43, 1121–1132.

Whittemore, R., and Knafl, K. (2005). The integrative review: updated methodology. J. Adv. Nurs 52, 546–553.

Yorks, L. (2008). What we know, what we don't know, what we need to know – integrative literature reviews are research. Hum. Resource Dev. Rev. 7(2), 139–141.

Postgraduate Thesis, Dissertation or Research Report: Different Formats and Flow From Title to Conclusion

Aceme Nyika

Graduate Support, Research and Innovation Department, University of Pretoria, Pretoria, South Africa.

Correspondence: nyikaa@yahoo.com

https://doi.org/10.21775/9781910190753.07

Abstract

Postgraduate qualifications that have a research component are awarded after examination of a write-up that contributes partially or wholly to the respective qualifications. The final write-ups are referred to as theses, dissertations or research reports depending on the level of the postgraduate qualification. The terminology also depends on the geographical regions; for instance, European countries tend to use terminology that is different from the USA, while in Africa there seems to be different terminologies based on the colonial history of individual countries. However, there are also variations within certain countries, depending on guidelines or policies of specific academic institutions.

In this article, issues that have a bearing on flow of arguments from title to conclusion of postgraduate theses, dissertations and research reports are unpacked. The main point being made is that there should be coherent flow of arguments from title of a research write-up to conclusion regardless of the format used.

Introduction

Terminology pertaining to write-ups tends to be used differently and interchangeably from one institution, country or region to another. Thus, the terminology may not be clearly defined even in institutional policy documents and regulations. However, it is important to have clarity of the expected end product of an academic programme so that students and their supervisors know what they have to aim to produce at the end of the programme. Such clarity will help the students and supervisors to figure out issues related to scope and depth of the research project upfront at the proposal development stage. The clarity will also minimize confusion about format of write-ups.

Terminology

In general, theses are write-ups for academic postgraduate doctorate degrees which are either PhD or professional degrees. A dissertation is generally for a master's or MPhil degree. However, in the USA the term dissertation is used for postgraduate doctorate degrees (PhD and professional degrees). Research reports are for the lowest category of postgraduate qualifications which include postgraduate honours degrees and postgraduate diplomas. Whereas different formats of theses for postgraduate doctorate degrees have emerged, dissertations and research reports have generally remained as monographs that have been used traditionally.

Thesis

The terms thesis, dissertation and research report are sometimes used differently in different parts of the world. In some cases, the terms are used interchangeably and inconsistently. For purposes of this chapter, definitions that are based mainly on the depth and scope of the research component of the degree programmes are used. The depth and scope of the research component is also reflected by the minimum permissible period within which a postgraduate degree programme can be completed. In addition, the weighting of the research component as depicted by the allocated credits also gives an indication of depth and scope that is expected for the postgraduate programmes.

The term thesis is widely used for write-ups that are derived from extensive research that constitute 100% of the requirements of an academic doctorate degree programme. In general, academic doctorate degree programmes are to be completed within a minimum period of 3 years for full-time candidates and 4 years for part-time candidates and are obtained after one has already acquired a relevant undergraduate degree as well as a postgraduate master's degree. Thus, the term thesis reflects the depth and scope of the research project conducted. Thesis requires the author to assimilate the findings of a comprehensive study and be able to theorize or synthesize new models or conceptions. In other words, the research should lead to significant contribution of new knowledge, and it is the university that determines at the proposal assessment stage whether or not the proposed research project would contribute something new and original to the body of existing knowledge.

Dissertations

Dissertation is used for write-ups that emanate from master's research projects. However, the contribution of the research component varies for different master's degrees; research may contribute 100% of the degree requirements in the case of a master's degree by research whereas it may contribute 50% or less in the case of masters by coursework plus research. To try and differentiate between the two types of master's degrees (by research or by coursework plus research), some institutions refer to the dissertation for the masters by research plus coursework as a mini-dissertation. However, some institutions use the term research report instead of mini-dissertation.

Research reports
Research reports are the lowest type of academic write-ups for examination purposes and they are for honours degrees and postgraduate diplomas. The scope and depth of research should be of levels lower than those for masters dissertations. The main aim of research reports is to demonstrate comprehension of the research process and the generally contribute about 20% of the requirements of the honours degree or postgraduate diploma concerned.

Formats of theses, dissertations and research reports
There are three main formats that can be used for theses, dissertations and research reports. The format that is based on chapters is the conventional format that has been used for academic purposes for centuries. Although some postgraduate students published their research findings in peer-reviewed journals in addition to packaging the findings in theses, dissertations or research reports for examination purposes, the majority of postgraduate students only focused on the examination process and did not publish their research findings. This meant that most postgraduate students tended to graduate and leave universities before publishing their research findings.

Thus, either the supervisors of the postgraduate research had to write up the research findings for publication or the findings gathered dust in theses, dissertations or research reports without being published in the mainstream peer-reviewed journals or books. Consequently, other formats of packaging research findings that accommodate examination requirements while at the same time promoting or encouraging publication of results by postgraduate students before graduating have been developed and introduced by various universities. The additional formats are the publication format and the submissible format. The three formats, namely (1) the conventional format, (2) the publication format and (3) the submissible format, are described in the following sections.

Format 1: conventional monograph
The monograph format enables a coherent story to be told from the topic through the research question and methodology to results and conclusion. There should be logical flow of arguments from the beginning to the end. The readers, especially the examiners, have to be convinced that the research question was answered appropriately through correct collection and analysis of relevant data.

General structure of a conventional monograph
The general structure of a conventional monograph can be considered to be composed of four main parts which are arranged as follows:

1. (a) administrative information;
2. (b) chapters that form the gist of the write-up;
3. (c) references;
4. (d) appendices.

The four parts are explained in more detail below.

Administrative information

Administrative information covers such details as details of the candidate, the research project being reported on and declaration that the work was honestly conducted by the candidate. The pages covering administrative information are numbered in Roman numerals and not in Arabic numerals. However, no page number should be written on the first page which is the page where the title of the project is stated. The common administrative information usually includes the following:

- title of the project (i, but not shown);
- candidate's declaration (ii);
- dedication* (iii);
- publications and presentations arising from the thesis (iv);
- abstract (check word limit permissible at your institution) (v);
- acknowledgements (vi);
- table of contents (vii);
- list of figures (viii);
- list of tables (ix);
- nomenclature (x).

Chapters

The conventional monograph has chapters that cover introduction, literature review, methods, results, discussion and conclusion. Chapters form the gist of the write-up. Depending on the scope, depth and nature of the research project being reported on, some chapters may be combined. For instance, for a research report emanating from a small research project introduction and literature review may be covered in the same chapter instead of having separate chapters. Similarly, discussion and conclusion may be covered in one chapter. In general, there are six chapters which cover the following:

- chapter 1: introduction;
- chapter 2: literature review;
- chapter 3: methods;
- chapter 4: results;
- chapter 5: discussion;
- chapter 6: conclusion.

Introduction, literature review and methods written up as part of the proposal can be used as the basis for chapters 1, 2 and 3, respectively. As the write-up is now reporting on what transpired in the study and the findings thereof, tense has to be changed from future tense to past tense, especially chapter 3 which covers the methods that were used. Thus, whereas in the introduction of the research proposal it may be stated that something will be done, in the introduction of the monograph the tense has to be changed to indicate that something was done.

---

*Dedication is optional.

It may be confusion to know what should be written in each of the chapters and how they can be linked to each other. Repetition compromises the quality of a write-up; hence it is important to know what should be covered in different chapters. The following sections give some tips that may guide candidates as they embark on writing different chapters.

Chapter 1: introduction
The introduction should put your study into context by giving a background and rationale for conducting the study. The introduction should start broadly, covering the big picture, and expounding the particular 'gap' in knowledge that forms the basis of your study. Thus, the introduction should be gradually narrowed down to the focus of the current study. For instance, one could start by explaining succinctly the global situation, followed by the continental situation and finally explain the national situation which may be the focus of one's research project.

Having given the background and rationale for the study, the statement of the problem or challenge to be addressed should be explicitly stated. The main research question that was addressed by the research project should then be stated. The main research question can then be converted into the aim or main objective of the project. For positivistic research projects the research hypothesis should be stated. The introduction should end with clearly stated specific objectives that the research project was set out to achieve. Clarity of the specific objectives can be enhanced by converting them into research questions. If there is a research hypothesis, it should be broken down into null and alternative hypotheses that can be tested.

Chapter 2: literature review
Research conducted in any field should be based on what is already known in order to address the reaming 'gaps' in knowledge. Thus, it is very unlikely that there would be nothing at all known in the field where research had to be conducted. It is therefore critical to critique what was already known when you embarked on your study and clearly explain what your own study aimed to address. That is done in a literature review. In other words, a literature review is not a mere compilation of studies that have been done in your research field but is a comprehensive critique of studies that have been done in your research field and a detailed justification for doing your study the way you did it. Your 'voice' as the author should be 'heard' through arguments that make use of findings reported by other researchers (found in literature) as premises for the arguments. Inability to paraphrase findings from literature and to use them in one's own arguments increases the chances of inadvertent plagiarism (Abasi Ali *et al*, 2006; Neville, 2012). Consequently, plagiarism is most likely to occur in the literature review section. Software such as Turnitin is used by most universities to help to identify possible plagiarized text in write-ups (Pankhurst and Moore, 2006). A detailed explanation of how one can go about doing a literature review is given in Chapter 6, which covers research proposal.

Chapter 3: methods
This chapter should explain the methods that were used to collect data and the analyses that were done. The chapter on methods which is in the proposal can be converted into

past tense as the study that was proposed would have been done now. If there were any changes to some aspects of the methods proposed in the research proposal then those methods should be amended accordingly.

Chapter 4: results
The chapter on results is arguably the most important chapter in a write-up because it captures what came out of the conducted study. The results section states the findings of the study and answers the research questions. Analysed data are presented and not raw data. The analysed results should be presented in a way that is easy to understand. Thus, if possible graphs or tables should be used and then explanations should be given in text. Even if data can be presented graphically or in tabular form, there should be concise text to walk the reader through the results. Figures and tables should not be dumped in the results section without any text to explain the points being conveyed.

Chapter 5: discussion
This chapter should discuss your own findings. In other words, the focus of the discussion should be your findings although they have to be compared and contrasted with other researchers' findings. Similarities and differences to other studies and possible reasons should be included. Consequently, the discussion chapter should start with your own findings from the current study, and then broaden the discussion to relate your findings to findings by other researchers. The chapter should not be another literature review, but a critical appraisal of your findings in light of the specific objectives and research questions that the current study sought to address. Fig. 7.1 shows a general structure of a chapter on discussion.

Chapter 6: conclusion
The final chapter focuses on conclusions drawn from the study. It is important for the main research question to be answered explicitly in this chapter. Recommendations

Figure 7.1 General structure of chapter on discussion.

based on the findings can also be included. However, it is possible to include conclusion and recommendations in the Discussion chapter instead of having a separate chapter, especially if the conclusion and recommendations are not very long.

References, referencing styles and reference management software
It has been noted that inability to cite references properly is one of the factors that may lead to unintentional plagiarism (Abasi Ali *et al*, 2006; Neville, 2012). All references cited in the whole write-up from the first to the last chapter should be listed at the end of the document. It is important to ensure that all cited references are included in the list. There are several referencing styles that can be used. The styles are to do with the way references are cited in text and how they are written in the reference list. For instance, when using the Vancouver referencing style, references cited are numbered in text in the order in which they appear for the first time and they are then listed in that order under list of references. In contrast, when using the Harvard referencing the names of the first three authors are cited in text and then all references cited in the whole document are listed in alphabetical order at the end of the document. Other referencing styles include APA, MLA and Chicago.

Reference management software programs help to manage references. They can be used to create one's own library, to cite references in text and to list cited references under reference list. Some reference management software such as Mendeley, Zotero and CiteUlike are freely available, while others, such as Endnote, RefWorks, Procite and Reference Manager, are commercially available. Most of the reference management software can manage the referencing styles so that the user simply chooses the style to be used in a document. Thus, the author does not have to manually format referencing styles.

Appendices
Documents that are not part of the main body of the thesis may be submitted as appendices. Such documents include ethical approvals, data collections tools, any important supplementary results, etc. Some universities may stipulate documents that should be included as appendices, whereas others leave it to the discretion of the students and supervisors.

Format 2: publication format
Most universities are now encouraging their masters and PhD students to aim to publish their research findings before they graduate. In fact, some universities now make it a requirement for PhD students to have published their research findings for them to be allowed to graduate. It means therefore that in addition to writing up theses, dissertations or research reports for examination purposes, postgraduate students may have to also write manuscripts for publication before the examination process. This may mean writing up the same research findings twice: firstly as manuscripts for publication in peer-reviewed journals and secondly as theses, dissertations or research reports for examination.

In order to streamline the process and prevent 'double workload' for students, a publication format of theses, dissertations and research reports has been developed and introduced by some universities. The publication format enables postgraduate students to submit published articles emanating from their postgraduate research for examination purposes. In other words, the published articles should cover research work done under the supervision of academic staff members appointed by the university after students have registered for their postgraduate degree programmes. This means that the students would not have to write conventional theses, dissertations or research reports, thus killing two birds with one stone.

The following are the general requirements for submission of published papers in lieu of the conventional theses, dissertations or research reports:

- The minimum number of published articles is one for a master's degree and three for a PhD degree.
- The articles must have been published after registration for the degree and must be derived from the research approved for the degree.
- The postgraduate student should be the first author, otherwise motivation explaining the role played by the student in the research has to be written and signed by the supervisor(s).
- The article(s) must have been published in reputable peer-reviewed journals approved by the university.
- There should be a written agreement signed by all co-authors indicating their consent for the student to use the published article for examination purposes.

The general structure of the publication format has four main parts, which are explained below.

Part A
Peripheral administrative information usually includes the following:

- title of the project (i, but not shown);
- candidate's declaration (ii);
- dedication* (iii);
- publications and presentations arising from the thesis (iv);
- abstract (check word limit permissible at your institution) (v);
- acknowledgements (vi);
- table of contents (vii);
- list of figures (viii);
- list of tables (ix);
- nomenclature (x).

Part B
Comprehensive integrated narrative.

Part C
Published article(s) (at least one for master's degree and at least three for PhD degree).

---

*Dedication is optional.

Part D
Overall concluding chapter.

Part E
Appendices.

Format 3: submissible manuscript format

In light of the fact that master's degree programmes take relatively shorter periods of time than PhD degree programmes, some universities have come up with a 'submissible manuscript' format for master's degrees that allows submission of manuscripts that are ready for publication but have not yet been published. In other words, masters students who initially may have intended to submit published articles can eventually submit manuscripts for examination as the process of publishing can be lengthy and unpredictable. Thus, in order to prevent efforts to publish from delaying the graduation of masters students, the 'submissible manuscript format' enables students to proceed to the examination process without having to revert to the conventional format which would mean 'double workload' in the form of the manuscript plus the conventional write-up (dissertation or research report).

The general structure of the submissible manuscript format has four main parts explained below:

Part A
Peripheral administrative parts.

Part B
Integrated introductory chapter.

Part C
Submissible manuscripts.

Part D
Overall concluding chapter.

Part E
Appendices.

Flow from topic to conclusion

Regardless of the format used, there should be clear flow of arguments from the beginning of the write-up to the end. It should be a continuous coherent 'story' that is supported by findings from your study that are interpreted in the context of findings from other researchers. Use of appropriate informative headings and subheadings helps to structure the write-up in such a way that points and arguments are communicated clearly. In the first chapter, an explanation of the overall structure of the whole write-up could be given so that the reader knows upfront what to expect. In addition, there should be a clear introduction in each chapter that outlines what is covered in that particular chapter.

Within each chapter, there should be logical flow from one section under a particular heading or subheading to the next. Each of the paragraphs that make up the sections should have one central point that is being conveyed. The first sentence of a paragraph should introduce the point. The introductory sentence is also referred to as the 'topic' sentence. Subsequent sentences should then explain the main point of the paragraph in succinct detail. It is critical to use transition words that enhance flow of arguments, ideas, or points from one sentence to the next. Examples of transition words include such words as consequently, additionally, however, nevertheless, subsequently, and others. Chronological transition words such as firstly, secondly, thirdly, etc., can also help to link sentences and enhance coherence. Finally, there should be a concluding sentence which sums up the gist of what has been conveyed by the paragraph.

References

Abasi Ali, R., Akbari, N., and Graves, B. (2006). Discourse appropriation, construction of identities, and the complex issue of plagiarism: ESL students writing in graduate school. J. Second Lang. Writ. *15*, 102–117.

Nivelle, C. (2012). Referencing: principles, practice and problems. RGUHS J. Pharm. Sci. *2*(2), 1–8.

Pankhurst, C., and Moore, E. (2006). Nipping plagiarism in the bud: using Turnitin to teach novice science writers how to paraphrase. Eur. Med. Writ. Assn. J. *15*, 125–128.

Research Integrity: The Obvious and the Less Obvious Dimensions

Aceme Nyika

Graduate Support, Research and Innovation Department, University of Pretoria, Pretoria, South Africa.

Correspondence: nyikaa@yahoo.com

https://doi.org/10.21775/9781910190753.08

Abstract

Research integrity is about the authenticity and trustworthiness of research. Research integrity has dimensions that may be relatively obvious and others that may not be so obvious. The obvious dimensions pertain to (i) fabrication of data, (ii) falsification of data, (iii) research methodology, (iv) plagiarism and (v) ethical issues. The not so obvious dimensions are to do with the reporting of findings as well as the environment in which the research is conducted and they include (a) authorship issues, (b) grant-related misconducts, (c) issues pertaining to collaboration, (d) intellectual property rights, (e) institutional and national environment in which research is conducted, (f) post-study issues and (g) other general cross-cutting issues. The different dimensions of research integrity pertain to various phases of the research process, starting from proposal writing through data collection, data analysis and interpretation of results to reporting of findings. Some aspects of research integrity go beyond the research process to the post-study period.

Failure to uphold high standards of research integrity can damage the image of various stakeholders that include individual researchers, families of the researchers concerned, research institutions, relevant government ministries and nations. Poor research integrity could also endanger the safety of the public as policies and or products may be based on flawed research findings. In addition, poor research integrity has financial implications which may be difficult to quantify fully. In this article, the different dimensions of research integrity are unpacked.

Introduction

Although research integrity may be defined in several different ways, most definitions are generally centred on virtuousness of players involved in research, especially the researchers themselves, as well as authenticity and trustworthiness of data and findings emanating from the research. Thus whereas some definitions of research integrity emphasise pertinent regulations or professional standards, other definitions tend to shift emphasis from adherence to rules and normative practices and focus on personality attributes of the researchers.

Historically, the importance of research integrity was brought to the fore by the unethical atrocities committed by the Nazis in Germany during the Second World War. The atrocities involved use of humans in experiments some of which were so dangerous that they caused deaths of innocent vulnerable people. In an effort to enhance research integrity and protect research participants, the Nuremburg code was developed in 1947. Thereafter, several other codes and guidelines such as the Declaration of Helsinki, the Council for International Organizations of Medical Sciences (CIOMS) guidelines and the Belmont Report were developed as part of efforts to further enhance research integrity. Research integrity goes beyond protection of humans, animals and the environment to include issues of authenticity as well as reporting of research findings.

In spite of the relatively increased awareness and existence of several codes or guidelines aimed at ensuring high standards of research integrity, cases of research activities that compromise research integrity have continued to occur globally. For instance, an unethical study was conducted at various NIH hospitals in the USA from 1932 to 1940. The study, now known as the Tuskegee scandal, was based on deliberately not treating poor black patients suffering from syphilis so as to investigate the natural pathogenesis of the disease from infection to death. Thus, infected people were not informed that they were not being treated, even after penicillin was shown to be an effective antibiotic to treat syphilis. In another example, a physicist based in the USA fabricated experimental results which he published in a total of 17 journal articles before the misconduct was uncovered (Service, 2002).

In the UK, the Alder Hey scandal involved removal of thousands of human body parts from deceased bodies without proper informed consent at 210 NHS hospitals from 1988 to 1995. One of the reasons for storing the body parts was for possible future research. Such kind of research which is based on biospecimens collected unethically compromises research integrity. In 1996 there was an epidemic outbreak of bacterial (meningococcal) meningitis in Tudun Wada, a very poor residential area in central Kano, Nigeria. As the Nigerian government was battling to contain the epidemic with the help of the MSF, a team of Pfizer researchers came into the country and joined the government and the MSF at the government hospital in Kano. It has been alleged that the Pfizer team was recruiting children into a trial of a drug called Trovan, or Trovafloxacin, which had never been administered to children orally (Ahmad, 2001). The Trovan clinical trial case resulted in legal actions in the USA and in Nigeria.

Another example of controversial studies that could tarnish the reputation of the players involved is an international collaborative study conducted in Malawi. The study involved various international researchers and international funding organizations (Mfutso-Bengu and Taylor, 2002, 2004; Rennie, 2004; Taylor et al. 2004; White et al.

2009; White, 2011). The controversy is due to the informed consent process which was based on partial disclosure of information to prospective participants. In order to study the back of eyes of study participants, it was necessary to remove the eyes from deceased children for ophthalmoscopic examination. Parents of the deceased Malawian children were not informed explicitly that eyes would be removed and replaced with artificial ones. Whereas the relevant ethics committee in the USA did not approve the study because of the proposed partial disclosure, the Malawian ethics committee approved the study and it was conducted without explicit disclosure of information upfront. One of the researchers pointed out that parents of the deceased were to be informed 'after the event' (Mfutso-Bengu and Taylor, 2002)).

As China's levels of publications have increased (Qui, 2015), up to 80% of clinical trial data in China were reported to be fraudulent (Woodhead, 2016). Focusing on research conducted in various countries, a case study conducted by Higgins *et al.* (2016) revealed that 17% of manuscripts submitted to a particular medical journal had plagiarized text. A wide range of possible underlying factors include the following: (i) ability to detect bad research may be improving, (ii) reporting of bad research may be increasing, (iii) cases of bad research may be increasing and (iv) the volume of research being conducted globally is increasing, hence cases of bad research may be increasing proportionally (Service, 2002; Titus *et al.*, 2008; Ana *et al.*, 2013; Higgins *et al.*, 2016; Pupovac *et al.*, 2016; Breen, 2016; Woodhead, 2016).

Although the proportion of research studies that violate research integrity may be relatively small compared with studies conducted properly, the bad research has potential to tarnish and overshadow the good research. However, it has been shown that many cases of research misconduct are still not being reported for various reasons (Titus *et al.*, 2008). Consequently, research integrity has increasingly become a very critical issue in research globally.

It is therefore critical for players involved in research to make concerted efforts not only to sensitive each other about research integrity but also to conduct empirical research on research integrity so as to come up with evidence-based mechanisms of preventing, detecting and/or dealing with research misconducts. Fig. 8.1 shows an overview of the obvious and the subtle dimensions of research integrity.

Obvious dimensions of research integrity

Fabrication of data

Fabrication of data means that fictitious data are 'created' or 'cooked' by the researchers so as to support a certain research hypothesis. Creation of data can be done at the data collection stage. The 'raw' data created may then be analysed as if they were genuine data. A simple example is a researcher who may complete several survey questionnaires so that it seems as if several people participated in the survey. The completed survey questionnaires would provide raw data which would be subsequently analysed as if the questionnaires were completed by genuine research participants.

Fabrication of data can also occur at the data analysis stage. At this stage, 'analysed' data are created. Using the example of a survey given above, fabrication at the analysis

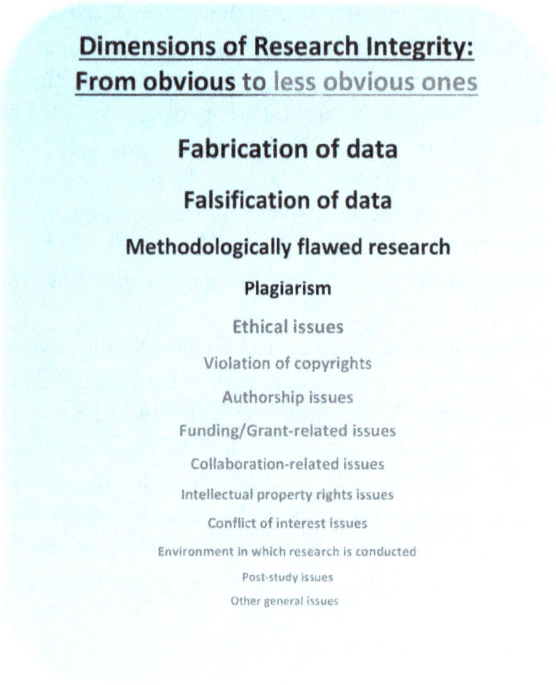

Dimensions of Research Integrity:
From obvious to less obvious ones

Fabrication of data

Falsification of data

Methodologically flawed research

Plagiarism

Ethical issues

Violation of copyrights

Authorship issues

Funding/Grant-related issues

Collaboration-related issues

Intellectual property rights issues

Conflict of interest issues

Environment in which research is conducted

Post-study issues

Other general issues

Figure 8.1 Dimensions of research integrity from the obvious ones to the less obvious ones.

stage could involve creation of prevalence percentages that are not based on any completed questionnaires. For example, a dishonest researcher could make up percentages of 'respondents' that supposedly gave specific responses.

Falsification of data

Falsification of data is the modification of existing data so that the data support a research hypothesis that the researcher wants to prove. Thus, data are not 'created' from scratch as is the case with fabrication, but there is manipulation of either the actual data collected and or the data collection procedures. Using the same example of a survey given above, a dishonest researcher may exclude questionnaires that give responses which do not seem to support the researcher's preferred research hypothesis. In a clinical trial of a medical drug, falsification of data may involve deliberately not reporting or recording serious adverse events caused by the drug so as to make it appear to have a good safety profile. Thus, the researcher does not create data, but manipulates the data collection process so as to end up with data that support a certain outcome.

Methodological issues

Research has to be methodologically sound for findings emanating from it to be regarded as credible. Peer researchers, policy makers, private sector, public sector, the general public and any other stakeholders expect research findings to be credible and free of flaws. Such research findings can only be derived from research that employs appropriate research methodologies to answer specific research questions.

Wrong research methodologies lead to wrong data collection methods, which in turn lead to data analyses methods that do not answer the research question. Consequently, wrong conclusions and recommendations may be made. Thus it is critical for researchers to be knowledgeable about research methodologies in order to determine the most appropriate methodology to answer specific research questions. It means therefore that it is advantageous for one to have broad knowledge of various research methodologies even though one may be an expert in a particular methodology.

If a researcher conducts research which is methodologically flawed, the reputation of various stakeholders may be tarnished. The stakeholders include the researcher himself/herself, the institution(s) to which the researcher is affiliated, the country where the researcher is based and the organization funding the research. If the findings based on flawed research methodology have been published, the reputation of the publisher of the flawed findings is also at stake.

Conduction of research that is methodologically flawed is a waste of resources as the outcomes would not be practically useful. If such a study involved human participants, it means that the efforts and goodwill of research participants were in vain. Another aspect of methodologically flawed research is the irreproducibility of the findings, which leads to further wastage of resources. This is because other researchers may unsuspectingly use the flawed findings as a basis for further studies only to find out that the findings reported by previous researchers are not reproducible.

Plagiarism

Plagiarism is use of other people's words or ideas without acknowledging the people who originally came up with those words or ideas. Plagiarism can be committed deliberately or inadvertently. Although intentional plagiarism may be rare, it still occurs to some extent. For instance, one researcher knowingly plagiarized someone else's complete PhD thesis (Lanegran, 2004). However, some cases of plagiarism may be arguably unintentional. For instance, quoting words verbatim without putting them in quotation marks is plagiarism even if a reference from which the direct quotation was obtained is cited. Thus, simply citing the reference without putting the words in quotation marks is not adequate.

To avoid plagiarizing, direct quotations must have (i) quotation marks to indicate that the words were taken verbatim and (ii) the reference from which the quotation was obtained (with exact page numbers where the quoted words can be found). Failure to paraphrase properly may lead to plagiarizing inadvertently. In other words, improper citation and referencing is tantamount to plagiarism. A case of plagiarism that involved a supervisor and his PhD student (Beyers *et al.*, 2007) could arguably be regarded as an example of such cases of inadvertent plagiarism. Another factor that may lead to inadvertent plagiarism is inability to differentiate between 'common knowledge' that does not necessarily need to be referenced and points, ideas or words that should be referenced.

Plagiarism can be detected on the basis of changes in the writing style. Thus, inconsistencies in the writing styles may be due to plagiarized materials obtained from various sources that have different writing styles. For instance, legal documents may have different writing styles from policy documents or journal articles. There are several software programs that can detect plagiarism in a document. The software would highlight parts of a document that are similar to parts of other documents that are in the public domain. Most institutions of higher education obtain institutional licences that enable their students and staff members to use particular plagiarism detection software.

Ethical issues

Research activities may affect people, animals, vegetation and the environment directly or indirectly. In an effort to ensure that research activities do not violate ethical principles, most countries have various types of ethics committees that review and approve research projects before they can be implemented. There are human ethics committees that review research projects that involve humans, animal ethics committees that review research projects that involve animals and biosafety committees that review projects that may affect the environment. Various ethical principles are used to review proposals for research that has a bearing on humans, animals or the environment.

For instance, for research involving humans the main ethical principles used are the principles of autonomy, beneficence, non-maleficence and justice. The principle of autonomy stipulates that human beings have a right to self-determination hence they should make autonomous and voluntary decisions whether to participate in research or not. The principle of beneficence stipulates that researchers should always ensure that research participants are treated as ends in themselves and not as means to some scientific end, hence ultimately there should be potential benefit to research participants and their communities. The principle of non-maleficence emphasizes the need to ensure that research activities do not cause harm to people participating. The principle of justice stipulates that there must be fairness in the recruitment of participants.

For research involving animals, the principle of the triple R, which stands for 'Replace', 'Reduce' and 'Refine', is used. The triple R principle means that (i) animals should always be replaced with other alternatives (e.g. cell culture, simulations, etc.) if possible, (ii) if not possible to replace animals then the numbers of the animals used should be reduced to the minimum required to answer the research question and (iii) methodologies and handling of animals should always be refined in order to minimize suffering of the animals (Nyika, 2009).

Approvals

Relevant approvals should be obtained before research proposals can be implemented. In addition to ethical approvals from the human, animal and or environmental committees, it may be necessary to obtain other pertinent approvals depending on the nature of the research and the collaborators involved. For instance, approvals from any collaborating institutions where data would be collected should be obtained. For some sensitive studies such as genomic research, approvals from some arm of government may be required in some countries.

Conducting research without the relevant approvals is a misconduct which compromises research integrity. Another subtle form of misconduct is deviation from the approved proposal without appropriate approval for the deviation. If the approvals given are valid for certain specified periods of time, it is unethical to continue the research without renewal of the approvals.

Informed consent

According to the principle of autonomy, people who participate in research should do so voluntarily after giving informed consent. For informed consent to be valid, prospective participants should be given all the important information about the research that is to be conducted. The information should include any known potential risks, any potential benefits and what participation will entail. The information should be written in a document that should be given to the prospective participant. The information provided to prospective participants should be easy to understand and should exclude unnecessary technical terms that do not enhance comprehension. Researchers should explain what the intended research is about orally in addition to providing written explanations. Prospective participants should be given chances to ask questions.

Conflict of interest

Conflict of interest means that there is a potential for the researcher to be biased. There are examples of researchers who were influenced by conflicts of interests and were biased in reporting their research findings. Unfortunately such biased findings may have far-reaching repercussions, especially in the medical field. One example is a study that was reported to link the vaccine for measles, mumps and rubella (MMR) to autism but was eventually found to be highly suspicious because the author stood to gain financially by portraying the MMR vaccine to be unsafe (Deer, 2011). Unfortunately, safety concerns continued to compromise public acceptance even after the conflict of interest of the author had been exposed (Freed *et al*, 2010). Another study that was discredited due to financial conflict of interest was the clinical trial of an antipsychotic medical treatment that was linked to pharmaceutical company that was intending to commercialize the treatment (Robbins *et al.*, 2011).

However, conflicts of interest in research may be of different forms apart from the financial one. Some examples include marking a research report, dissertation or thesis of a relative or close collaborator, reviewing a research proposal of a relative or close collaborator and reviewing a manuscript of a relative or close collaborator. Thus conflict of interest should be considered by ethics committees when they review research proposals, by academic institutions in their examination processes and funding organizations when they review grant applications.

Not so obvious dimensions of research integrity

Authorship issues

Criteria for selecting eligible authors

The criteria for one to be considered to be an author of an article reporting research findings are controversial and debatable. In some cases, the issue of authorship is not tackled upfront and becomes a thorny issue when researchers get to the point of publishing their research findings. Some research institutions have put in place institutional policies on authorship, although implementation of the policies may be ineffective in some cases.

In order to promote research integrity, researchers should agree on the criteria for authorship before commencement of the research. The criteria should clearly explain how one qualifies to be an author and how the position of the author in the list of authors is to be determined. In other words, the criteria should answer the following questions:

- What are the conditions for one to be the first author on an article?
- What are the criteria for selecting the other co-authors?
- How is the order of the co-authors determined?
- What are the conditions for someone to be acknowledged?

The guidelines developed by the International Committee of Medical Journal Editors (ICMJE) stipulate that authorship should be based on the following four criteria:

1. 'Substantial contributions to the conception or design of the work; or the acquisition, analysis, or interpretation of data for the work; AND
2. Drafting the work or revising it critically for important intellectual content; AND
3. Final approval of the version to be published; AND
4. Agreement to be accountable for all aspects of the work in ensuring that questions related to the accuracy or integrity of any part of the work are appropriately investigated and resolved.'

In order for one to be regarded as an author, one should meet all the four criteria for authorship. If one does not meet all of the four criteria but meets some of them, then one should be acknowledged. In addition to being accountable for the parts of the work he or she has done, an author should know the other co-authors involved and their specific contributions. It is important not to exclude people who deserve to be authors or to be acknowledged. It is also equally important not to include undeserving people as authors or to acknowledge them. Below are some categories of people who tend to be inappropriately excluded or included.

- People who are usually unfairly excluded:
  - students;
  - junior researchers;
  - deserving collaborators.
- People who are usually included when they do not deserve to be included:
  - bosses;
  - influential collaborators;
  - 'ghost' authors;
  - 'parasitic' authors.

Spinning results

Spinning of results is not fabrication or falsification per se, but is a way of presenting and conveying results in such a way that certain conclusions can be made. Salient details which could weaken the evidence for the preferred conclusions may be deliberately left out. Various empirical studies have shown that spinning tends to be done in abstract, results, discussion and conclusion sections (Boutron *et al.*, 2010; Lockyer, 2013).

Publishing same data more than once

One other dimension of research integrity which is not usually brought to the fore is publication of the same research findings more than once. Unscrupulous researchers can deliberately publish the same research findings in two or more journals. Slightly different titles would be used so that the publications seem to be different. In order to minimize chances of the duplication being discovered, text in the introduction, literature review, methodology, results and discussion sections of the duplicated papers is worded differently, otherwise the duplication could be picked up as plagiarism. Cases of publication of the same findings more than once have been discovered in various fields (Blancett *et al.*, 1995; Bailey, 2002; Errami and Garner, 2008; Errami *et al.*, 2008; Kim *et al.*, 2008; Lariviere and Gingras, 2010)

Funding/grant-related misconducts

Misappropriation of funds

One type of misconduct is misappropriation of research funds. Funds may be misappropriated for research-related purposes such as funding activities that were not approved by the funders. A worse form of misappropriation of research funds is use of funds for personal activities that are not research related at all.

Double-dipping

Double-dipping means obtaining funds from more than one source for exactly the same research project. Thus, the researcher receives excess funding, which means that the surplus funds can be used for something else without the knowledge of the funders. Progress reports required by the funders would still be submitted as per the grant agreements, but the reports would be on the same project. The requirement for researchers to disclose the source of funding when research findings are published helps to prevent double-dipping, provided the researchers do publish their findings. A requirement to submit supporting financial documents (e.g. invoices, receipts, etc.) together with reports to funders goes a long way in preventing double-dipping.

Not accounting for research grants through reports

Although accounting for research funds through progress reports is almost always a condition for grants, some researchers fail to submit such mandatory reports. This is usually the case if the recipients are subgrantees who have to report to a main grantee who was awarded the grant by the funders.

Issues pertaining to collaboration

Collaboration in research may be between researchers belonging to the same or different departments, institutions or countries. Issues that need to be tackled upfront are more or less the same at the different levels of collaboration but may differ in terms of their complexity. This is because of possible heterogeneity of pertinent policies or guidelines at different institutions or in different countries. Secondly, the number of researchers and size of research projects involved in collaborations tend to be greater at international levels than at institutional levels.

Power differentials

Power differentials in collaborative projects may lead to challenges that may compromise the integrity of the research at the end of the day. If there are no clear decision making procedures put in place upfront decisions may end up being made by influential members of the collaborative team without much input from the weak members.

'Parasitic collaborators'

Some members of collaborative groups may be parasitic in that they may not contribute much in terms of development of the research proposal, implementation of the projects and reporting of research findings but they may still benefit by virtue of them being part of the collaboration. Such parasitic researchers may be included merely to satisfy a certain requirement stipulated by the funders. For instance, one condition of funding may be that a collaborative consortium must be made up of institutions based in certain global regions. Thus, certain researchers and their institutions may be included merely to satisfy the conditions set by the funders and not because the researchers would have contributed to the development of the research project.

Sharing of specimens and data

One of the potentially thorny issues surrounding collaborative research projects is the issue of sharing specimens and data. Although various researchers and their institutions may be involved in the collection of specimens and generation of data, the issue of ownership and sharing thereafter may be problematic. Whereas during the course of the study all collaborative partners may have access to specimens and data, the modalities of access after the lifespan of the collaborative project may not be clear and straightforward. In some cases, the institution of the leading applicant, that is the main principal investigator of the collaborative study, ends up with the custody of specimens and data either by default or by design. The other collaborative partners may not have access to the specimens and data after the collaborative project has ended.

Other issues surrounding collaboration

The other issues surrounding collaboration that could compromise research integrity are authorship issues and intellectual property rights (IPR) issues. It is critical for these issues to be tackled upfront because if several departments, institutions and or countries are involved they may have different policies (or no policies at all) pertaining to those issues. In addition, some funders have conditions that pertain to authorship and IPR issues, hence compatibility with policies of collaborating institutions may have to be unpacked and sorted out upfront.

Intellectual property rights and patents

As global economies are increasingly becoming knowledge driven (Bastalich, 2010), intellectual property rights issues are correspondingly becoming critical. Intellectual property rights are based on intellectual assets, which are creations of the human mind which can potentially be turned into useful tangible or intangible products. If one protects one's intellectual asset through a legal process, then one has intellectual property rights over the asset. Intellectual property rights can cover inventions in all fields of human endeavour. A patent is a legal protection of an invention for a specified period of time in specified country or countries. Thus, a patent protects an inventor for a certain period of time (usually up to 20 years) during which the inventor can develop the invention to commercial products. There are two broad categories of intellectual rights as shown in Table 8.1. Also shown in Table 8.1 are intellectual assets which cannot be patented.

Environment in which research is conducted

The environment in which researchers conduct their research has a bearing on the quality and integrity of the research. Thus institutions have to ensure that they create environments that are conducive to research of high integrity. It means therefore that such aspects of research environment as infrastructure, policies, quality control procedures and support programmes have to be such that they enable and promote research of the highest possible quality.

Research institutions have to strive to provide state-of-the-art infrastructure so as to enable researchers to conduct cutting-edge research without hindrances associated with outdated equipment. Basic but critical needs such as availability of electricity, internet, water and adequate space should be catered for. Polices that pertain to management of grants acquired on the institutional platform, ownership of specimens and data, sharing of specimens and data, collaboration within the institution, collaboration with other institutions and IPR have to be in place.

In order to ensure total quality management of research conducted on the institutional platform, such mechanisms as institutional ethics committees, peer-review procedures, supervision of research, proper storage facilities for specimens and data and research capacity building programmes should not only be established but should also be continuously

Table 8.1 Different types of intellectual property rights and copyrights

Industrial property rights	Copyrights	Not patentable
Industrial designs	Literary works	Mathematical methods
Patents of inventions	Artistic works	Scientific theories
Trade and service marks	Computer software	Plant varieties
Trade secrets	Electronic databases	Animal hybrids
		Genomic sequences
		Discoveries

reviewed. In addition, provision of various software that could help researchers to collect data, analyse data and report findings could go a long way in strengthening the research capacity of researchers and the quality of their research outputs. Examples of the software include data management software, data analysis software (for both quantitative and qualitative data), reference management software and plagiarism detection software.

Post-study issues

Reputation of researchers is not only affected by what transpires during the course of the research but can also be affected by pertinent post-study issues. For instance, if a study was largely community based and there is no effort to feedback to the community after the study is completed the community may feel that they were 'exploited' by the researchers. Thus, the community may then perceive the researchers as being exploitative and may not want to participate in future studies.

Another post-study issue is to do with access to products or interventions derived from the research. Research participants and the communities from which they were drawn may feel short-changed if there are no efforts to ensure that they can benefit to some feasible extent from the outcomes of the research they participated in.

Other general issues

Over-researching certain communities or geographical locations

Research integrity can potentially be negatively affected by some general issues that may be indirectly associated with the research. One such issue is the perception of targeting particular communities or geographical locations to the extent that the communities or locations may be considered to have been over-researched. However, there could be divergent schools of thought regarding this issue. One school of thought may be that the communities or locations concerned actually benefit from the research conducted, while another school of thought may be that the communities or locations are exploited.

Setting research agenda

The issue of setting of research agenda can be controversial, especially if there is collaboration involving developed and developing countries. The question that may be asked is whether or not the research objectives that tend to be set by funding organizations match the needs of the other players involved. Researchers should be addressing the pressing needs of the communities and countries where the research is conducted. Thus, it is important for research agendas to be derived from the needs of the researched communities.

References

Ahmad, K. (2001). Drug company sued over research trial in Nigeria. Lancet 358, 815.
Ana, J., Koehlmoos, T., Smith, R., and Yan, L.L. (2013). Research misconduct in low- and middle-income countries. PLOS Med. *10*, e1001315. https://doi.org/10.1371/journal.pmed.1001315
Bailey, B.J. (2002). Duplicate publication in the field of otolaryngology-head and neck surgery. Otolaryngol. Head Neck Surg. *126*, 211–216.
Bastalich, W. (2010). Knowledge economy and research innovation. Stud. High. Educ. 35, 845–857.

Beyers, N., Enarson, D.A., Pierard, C., and Chan-Yeung, M. (2007). Response to a case of plagiarism in the International Journal of Tuberculosis and Lung Disease. Int. J. Tuberc. Lung Dis. *11*, 473–473.

Blancett, S.S., Flanagin, A., and Young, R.K. (1995). Duplicate publication in the nursing literature. Image J. Nurs. Sch. *27*, 51–56.

Boutron, I., Dutton, S., Ravaud, P., and Altman, D.G. (2010). Reporting and interpretation of randomized controlled trials with statistically nonsignificant results for primary outcomes. JAMA *303*, 2058–2064.

Breen, K.J. (2016). Research misconduct: time for a re-think? Intern. Med. J. *46*, 728–733. https://doi.org/10.1111/imj.13075

Deer, B. (2011). How the case against the MMR vaccine was fixed. BMJ *342*, c5347. https://doi.org/10.1136/bmj.c5347

Deer, B. (2011). Secrets of the MMR scare. How the vaccine crisis was meant to make money. BMJ *342*, c5258. https://doi.org/10.1136/bmj.c5258

Errami, M., and Garner, H. (2008). A tale of two citations. Nature *451*, 397–399. https://doi.org/10.1038/451397a

Errami, M., Hicks, J.M., Fisher, W., Trusty, D., Wren, J.D., Long, T.C., and Garner, H.R. (2008). Déjà vu – a study of duplicate citations in Medline. Bioinformatics *24*, 243–249.

Freed, G.L., Clark, S.J., Butchart, A.T., Singer, D.C., and Davis, M.M. (2010). Parental vaccine safety concerns in 2009. Pediatrics *125*, 654–659. https://doi.org/10.1542/peds.2009-1962

Higgins, J.R., Lin, F.C., and Evans, J.P. (2016). Plagiarism in submitted manuscripts: incidence, characteristics and optimization of screening – case study in a major specialty medical journal. Research Integrity and Peer Review *1*, 13. https://doi.org/10.1186/s41073-016-0021-8

International Committee of Medical Journals Editors (ICMJE). Available at: http://www.icmje.org/recommendations/browse/roles-and-responsibilities/defining-the-role-of-authors-and-contributors.html (accessed 6 February 2017).

Kim, S.Y., Hahm, C.K., Bae, C.W., and Cho, H.M. (2008). Duplicate Publications in Korean medical journals indexed in KoreaMed. J. Korean Med. Sci. *23*, 131–133. https://doi.org/10.3346/jkms.2008.23.1.131

Lanegran, K. (2004). Fending off a plagiarist. The Chronicle of Higher Education. Available at: http://www.chronicle.com/article/Fending-Off-a-Plagiarist/44680 (accessed 22 November 2016).

Lariviere, V., and Gingras, Y. (2010). On the prevalence and scientific impact of duplicate publications in different scientific fields (1980–2007). J. Doc. *66*, 179–190.

Lockyer, S., Hodgson, R., Dumville, J.C., and Cullum, N. (2013). 'Spin' in wound care research: the reporting and interpretation of randomized controlled trials with statistically non-significant primary outcome results or unspecified primary outcomes. Trials *14*, 371. https://doi.org/10.1186/1745-6215-14-371

Mfutso-Bengu, J.M., and Taylor, T.E. (2002). Ethical jurisdictions in biomedical research. Trends Parasitol. *18*, 231–234.

Mfutso-Bengu, J.M., and Taylor, T.E. (2004). Response to Rennie: Is there a place for benevolent deception? Trends Parasitol. *20*,164.

Nyika, A. (2009). Animal research ethics in Africa: an overview. Acta Trop. *112* (Suppl. 1), S48–52. https://doi.org/10.1016/j.actatropica.2009.07.021

Pupovac, V., Prijic´-Samarzija, S., and Petrovecki, M. (2016). Research misconduct in the Croatian scientific community: a survey assessing the forms and characteristics of research misconduct. Sci. Eng. Ethics 23(1), 165–181. https://doi.org/10.1007/s11948-016-9767-0

Qiu, J. (2015). Safeguarding research integrity in China. Natl. Sci. Rev. *2*, 122–125. https://doi.org/10.1093/nsr/nwv002

Rennie, S. (2004). Is there a place for benevolent deception? Trends Parasitol. *20*, 163. https://doi.org/10.1016/j.pt.2004.01.007

Robbins, B.D., Higgins, M., Fisher, M., and Over, K. (2011). Conflicts of interest in research on antipsychotic treatment of pediatric bipolar disorder, temper dysregulation disorder, and attenuated psychotic symptoms syndrome: exploring the unholy alliance between big pharma and psychiatry. J. Psychol. Issues Organ Cult. *1*(4), 32–49. https://doi.org/10.1002/jpoc.20039/pdf

Service, R.F. (2002). Scientific misconduct. Bell Labs fires star physicist found guilty of forging data. Science *298*, 30–31. https://doi.org/10.1126/science.298.5591.30

Taylor, T.E., Fu, W.J., Carr, R.A., Whitten, R.O., Mueller, J.S., Fosiko, N.G., Lewallen, S., Liomba, N.G., Molyneux, M.E., and Mueller, J.G. (2004). Differentiating the pathologies of cerebral malaria by postmortem parasite counts. Nat. Med. *10*, 143–145. https://doi.org/10.1038/nm986

Titus, S.L., Wells, J.A., and Rhoades, L.J. (2008). Repairing research integrity. Nature *453*, 980–982. https://doi.org/10.1038/453980a

White, V.A., Lewallen, S., Beare, N.A., Molyneux, M.E., and Taylor, T.E. (2009). Retinal pathology of pediatric cerebral malaria in Malawi. PLOS ONE *4*, e4317. https://doi.org/10.1371/journal.pone.0004317

White, V.A. (2011). Malaria in Malawi: inside a research autopsy study of pediatric cerebral malaria. Arch. Pathol. Lab. Med. *135*, 220–226. https://doi.org/10.1043/1543-2165-135.2.220

Woodhead, M. (2016). 80% of China's clinical trial data are fraudulent, investigation finds. BMJ *355*, i5396. https://doi.org/10.1136/bmj.i5396

Professional Doctorate Degrees: How Do They Differ From Conventional PhD Degrees?

Aceme Nyika

Graduate Support, Research and Innovation Department, University of Pretoria, Pretoria, South Africa.

Correspondence: nyikaa@yahoo.com

https://doi.org/10.21775/9781910190753.09

Abstract

Whereas the conventional PhD degree is generally meant for candidates aspiring to become academics and researchers in academic or research environments, the professional doctorate degree which has emerged recently is meant for practising professionals who may already be in senior positions and have gained extensive experience in their fields of specialization. Consequently, research topics for professional doctorate degrees emanate from practical professional practice and may be aimed at addressing specific practical challenges encountered in real-life settings. The same minimum requirement stipulated for a PhD, which is to make an original contribution to the body of knowledge, is applicable to professional doctorate degrees. The main difference is that the new knowledge generated should have direct relevance and applicability to the candidates' specific professional field. This article unpacks professional doctorate degrees and articulates some of the potential challenges.

Introduction

Globally, doctoral education has been undergoing transition influenced by the changing economies of knowledge and practice. The transition led to the emergence of professional doctorate degrees in the early 1990s. Whereas the conventional Doctor of Philosophy (PhD) degrees are based mainly on academic research, the professional doctorate degrees are centred on professional practice. However, one common feature of the two types of academic doctorate degrees is that they are universally considered to be the highest levels of academic qualifications which are awarded on the basis of examination of theses that contribute significantly to the body of academic knowledge. The two academic doctorate degrees should be distinguished from honorary doctorate degrees which are not based on theses but are awarded in recognition of outstanding contribution to society.

Professional doctorate degrees have spread to universities in many developed countries including Australia (Lee et al., 2009), UK, USA, Canada (Chiteng Kot and Hendel, 2011) and New Zealand (Subramanian and Thomson). The growth and spread of professional doctorate degrees could be partially attributed to the increasing use of technology in practice which has led to the expansion of knowledge underlying practice. In general, professional doctorate degrees have been offered in such fields as medicine, dentistry, engineering, law, psychiatry, business administration and education.

However, not many universities in developing countries in general, and in Africa in particular, are offering professional doctorate degrees. This is in spite of the fact that most African countries are aiming to increase numbers of doctorate graduates produced by universities. For instance, South Africa aims to increase the national doctoral output from 1 400 to 6000 per annum by the year 2030 (National Planning Commission, 2012). As professional doctorate degrees enable professionals to continue working while using professional work for academic purposes, it could be an effective way to attract professionals to obtain doctorate degrees.

This article gives an overview of professional doctorate degrees and covers the definition, general structure, entry requirements, supervision, thesis formats and examination of professional doctorate degrees. The articles ends with some potential challenges that could be associated with professional doctorate degrees.

Definition of professional doctorate degree

A professional doctorate degree is a practice-based doctoral degree which is aimed at equipping candidates with the ability to apply as well as generate knowledge in the workplace. Thus, the main aim of the degree is not to prepare candidates for academic careers but to strengthen their professional expertise through an intensive research process that yields new knowledge. In other words, the professional doctorate degree is designed to incorporate research-derived knowledge into the professional practice of experienced professional practitioners. As the research directly relates to, and is rooted in, the professional practice of the candidate, the output should not only contribute to knowledge but have a significant impact on the specific professional practice.

General structure of professional doctorate degrees

In general, professional doctorate degrees are composed of practical work that may have been done as part of a candidate's day-to-day professional duties. The degree is based entirely (100%) on the practical work. There may be some specific taught courses that candidates may be required to take but such courses do not contribute per se to the degree. Some institutions have mandatory core courses that have to be undertaken by all postgraduate students including professional doctorate degree students, but at some institution it is the supervisors who determine whether or not candidates have to undertake certain taught courses. Due to the dependency on the practical work of the candidate, professional doctorate degrees are usually on a part-time basis. Degree completion periods are around three years.

Entry requirements

A master's degree is the main entry requirement. However, in some special cases relevant experience may be considered in lieu of a master's degree provided a candidate has at least an undergraduate degree. In addition to the minimum academic qualifications, applicants may be required to submit a motivation and a synopsis of the research proposal which can be used to assess the potential ability of the candidate to undertake a professional doctorate degree. The research proposal may incorporate work that has already been done provided the work is related to the proposed thesis topic. Prospective supervisors may also be involved in the assessment process.

Supervision

Due to the dependency of the degree on practice, it may be necessary to have a 'professional' co-supervisor in addition to the 'academic' supervisor based at the institution where the candidate is registered for the professional doctorate degree. The decision to appoint a co-supervisor may be made by the academic supervisor and or by the relevant postgraduate committee that reviews the candidate's research proposal

Thesis formats

There are two main formats that are permissible for professional doctorate theses, the conventional monograph and publication format. However, the latter is generally recommended because the candidates, by virtue of having been academically active in their practice, are likely to have published journal articles which could be part of the doctorate thesis. For instance, in the medical field a medical practitioner may have been publishing case reports which collectively could contribute some new knowledge and inform practice or policy. The publication format enables published articles to form the main part of the thesis, accompanied by an integrated introductory narrative at the beginning and an overarching discussion chapter after the articles. If the conventional format is used, published articles should still be included but as appendices.

Examination

The examination process for professional doctorate degrees is the same as that for the conventional PhD degrees. In general, one internal examiner and two external examiners (one of whom should be an international examiner) should mark the final theses. Professional experts may be included as examiners in addition to traditional academic examiners. Some institutions have oral examinations (vivas) in addition to the thesis examination.

Potential challenges: completion rates and attrition risks

One of the main potential challenges is long completion periods because the professional doctoral degree students remain full-time employees when they enrol as part-time students. Thus, they may not create adequate time to work on their studies which could lead to prolonged degree completion periods. The long completion periods may be associated with high dropout rates.

Another potential challenge is limited supervisory capacity. For some professional fields the professional doctorate degrees are actually aimed at addressing critical shortages of professionals with doctorate degrees. Thus, getting suitably qualified supervisors could be a challenge. For instance, a requirement that an academic should have a doctorate degree in order to supervise a doctorate student may have to be waived in some cases so as to enable experienced professionals who may not have doctorate degrees to supervise doctorate students.

References

Chiteng Kot, F., and Hendel, D.D. (2011). Emergence and growth of professional doctorates in the United States, United Kingdom, Canada and Australia: a comparative analysis. Stud. Higher Educ. 37(3), 1–20.

Lee, A., Brennan, M., and Green, B. (2009). Re-imagining doctoral education: Professional Doctorates and beyond, High. Educ. Res. Dev. 28, 275–287. https://doi.org/10.1080/07294360902839883

National Planning Commission, (2012). National Development Plan: Vision 2030: Our future – Make it work. Pretoria: National Planning Commission. Available at: http://www.gov.za/issues/national-development-plan-2030 (accessed 15 March 2016).

Subramanian, J., and Thomson, W.M. (2016). The learning environment in professional doctorate and postgraduate dental education: a qualitative study. Eur. J. Dent. Educ. Available at: http://onlinelibrary.wiley.com/doi/10.1111/eje.12209/full (accessed 24 August 2017).

'Guys! Let Me Tell You About My PhD Supervisor': Postgraduate Supervision Practicalities and Approaches

10

Aceme Nyika

Graduate Support, Research and Innovation Department, University of Pretoria, Pretoria, South Africa.

Correspondence: nyikaa@yahoo.com

https://doi.org/10.21775/9781910190753.10

Abstract

Postgraduate supervision is critical in the development of resourceful and innovative professionals for the future. The development of student–supervisor environments that are conducive to effective learning requires an inclusive and participatory process that takes into account a wide range of characteristics of students being supervised on one hand and supervisors on the other. Due to power differentials in the student–supervisor relationships, students may not reveal some of their perceptions, challenges, expectations, shortcomings or other characteristics to their supervisors or university structures. In this paper, a hypothetical case study which captures a wide repertoire of pertinent issues surrounding doctoral student–supervisor relationships from different perspectives is presented. The case study shows that interpersonal relationships are dynamic and are affected by multiple factors, some of which are beyond the control of the students and or supervisors concerned. The author concludes therefore, that a 'one-size-fits-all' approach to postgraduate supervision is not always effective and is inadvisable.

Introduction

Postgraduate supervisors play a major role in doctoral studies; they guide the students from the point of registering for the PhD degree studies to the point of graduating. Murphy et al (2007) point out that there is duality in the role of supervisors which may create tension as on one hand the supervisors have to guide and train the doctoral students and on the other they have to ensure that the research findings and final write-up are of acceptable quality as per institutional requirements. The extent to which there is tension arguably depends mainly on the nature of the student–supervisor relationship. It is therefore critical that supervisors are aware of the potential tensions and proactively institute supervisory styles that help to mitigate the tensions. Although frequency of contact between supervisor and student is important (Pearson, 1996) it is the quality of the contacts that is more critical (Li and Searle 2007).

Empirical studies have shown that interpersonal relationships between doctoral students and their supervisors have a bearing on the overall quality of postgraduate supervision (Golde 2000; Marsh *et al.* 2002; Ives and Rowley 2005). It has been pointed out that power differentials between supervisors and students significantly influence the quality of supervision (Bartlett Mercer, 2000; Manathunga, 2007). It follows therefore that the effectiveness of some formal procedures aimed at eliciting information about the quality of supervision from supervised students may be compromised by such power differentials.

In this chapter, a case study is used to capture some complex and diverse challenges which may affect the quality of postgraduate supervision in general and student–supervisor relationships in particular. The case study is based on real-life events which occurred at African universities. The events have been interwoven into a single vignette in order to highlight the diversity of students' backgrounds, personality attributes and socio-economic circumstances on one hand and the diversity of supervisors' personalities and supervision styles on the other. The main purpose of the chapter is to argue for pragmatic supervision styles that take into account all the pertinent factors which have the potential to affect student–supervisor relationships and hence the quality of supervision.

Case study: 'Guys, let me tell you about my supervisor'

Six PhD students at International University (IU) had become close friends and had developed a habit of meeting to relax at the IU Students Union Recreation Hub on the last Friday night of every month. They would chat about various issues, including postgraduate studies, socio-economic life, career development matters, sexual relationships and current political affairs. On this Friday night, they were seated at their usual table on the far end of the Hub and Todd, a PhD student who is generally quiet and always drinks apple or orange juice, has raised an issue about his studies and how his supervisor is giving him a hard time. Todd explains that although his supervisor was initially 'nice and understanding' she has gradually become very 'unfriendly and too strict', giving him milestones to achieve within given deadlines. 'I now have a wife and a child, unlike when I started my PhD programme, and I cannot spend as much time on my studies as I used to do. My supervisor does not seem to care about my family responsibilities, yet this is the time when I really need her support and understanding. When I had to take days off to visit my twin brother who was seriously ill and was in hospital for several months she said I was not serious about my studies. All she is concerned about is the need to publish some results and to complete the PhD programme', said Todd as he uncharacteristically sipped on a cold beer.

'Eish!, it seems your supervisor has made you realize that beer can help you to de-stress neh!', retorted Fatso, the short and talkative PhD student who has completed data collection and is now concentrating on data analysis and writing up. 'Yoh!, mine is also crazy about this issue of publishing. My supervisor is always on my case and keeps yelling at me….."Fatso, you need to publish some results!" "Fatso, I want at least 3 papers from your work!" I have a life to live and have fun. All I want is to write up my thesis, pass, get a job and get on with my life. This business of publishing is not meant for me... I do not have the time. After five days of work I need to go out every weekend and have fun. My supervisor wants me to work even during weekends. Am I a prisoner with restricted freedom? No I am a free young man in a free country! That is why I just want to get the PhD thing out of the way so that I can be free. Get a job, get married and have fun without anyone nagging me about papers. Mixing PhD studies, marriage and family is a recipe for disaster. I have always told you guys; now see Todd has been forced to drink beer. Welcome to the club Todd!', said Fatso before he was interrupted by Marvellous, the well-spoken and confident PhD student in second year of her studies, 'No, that is not correct. One can be married and still be able to do one's PhD studies. It just depends on the individual student and his or her supervisor(s). What about mixing PhD studies with going out every weekend... is that not a recipe for disaster? One has to be able to manage one's time properly and have a work plan that is agreed on by the supervisors. Right from the beginning I discussed with my two supervisors what my overall plan is, which includes getting married by the end of my third year of studies'.

Marvellous' response seemed to evoke a lot of responses as several students shouted their responses. 'It can work for you because you are a lady and once you get married your husband will support you adequately and you can continue with your studies', shouted Todd who was surprisingly talkative and domineering on this Friday night. Fatso sprang up and shouted 'Unlike us male students, you ladies are treated leniently by most supervisors, especially if the supervisors are male'. At this point the discussion degenerated into loud chaotic noise. The female students were also physically on their feet shouting comments and questions most of which were unfortunately drowned in the loud noise. 'Fatso!...Fatso! as a PhD student you should know that any argument should be supported by empirical evidence. Do you have empirical evidence to support your statement? Even if there were some cases of gender-based favouritism, it would be wrong to generalize' shouted Marvellous with an emotional voice.

'Guys!, Guys!, I agree with Marvellous. Are you insinuating that performance of female students is lower than that of male students? One could also speculate that female supervisors favour male students. Or male supervisors favour male students. Supervisors are professional academics who carry out their duties ethically. In addition, universities have systems with checks and balances aimed at minimizing such unprofessional practices. It is all about having plans up front and discussing them with all stakeholders involved. I have a fiancé who is working and taking care of me and our two children. She is a lady and she is an excellent breadwinner. My parents and my fiancé's parents are also helping us in many ways. We discussed and agreed that I should focus on my studies full time instead of doing it part time. We agreed that once I finish my PhD studies and get a job then we can save money for a white wedding. I will invite all of you guys! It will be massive… glamorous…', said Blazo, who has always been teased by his friends as being a big baby who is spoon-fed by his relatives. 'Quiet! Quiet guys! Let's listen to our friends from foreign countries! They may think we do not like foreign students. Hey Blazo... enough about your fiancé', interjected Fatso, the 'monitor by default'.

'My two supervisors are different, my primary supervisor is like yours Fatso; his concerns do not go beyond my research findings and potential publications from my work. When I submit something to him to review, all I get as feedback are devastating negative comments which make me even more confused in terms of what I should do to improve my work. He enjoys using such words as 'superficial', 'rubbish', 'meaningless', 'shallow', 'muddled-up' and other negative words without explaining in what way my write-up is wrong. In contrast, my co-supervisor gives constructive feedback, but unfortunately most of my work has to be reviewed by my primary supervisor. Sometimes I get conflicting instructions from the two supervisors and I find it difficult to know whose instructions I should follow. My co-supervisor is so supportive that he takes time to ask about other aspects of my life like study permit, accommodation, financial status, my health and medical insurance. My co-supervisor does his best to help whenever he can, even offering me a lift in his car to the Immigration Offices to speed up the process of getting a study permit.', said Warisha, a foreign student in the third year of his PhD studies. At this point Nexus, who registered for her PhD five years ago, had a chance to tell others about her experiences; 'I think I should consider myself very lucky. My two supervisors are very supportive. They always liaise before having a meeting with me. All email correspondence regarding my PhD studies is seen by the three of us. We discussed and agreed on responsibilities of each one of us and the time frame of the whole programme', explained Nexus.

'Guys, we even have details of who will review what when it comes to the writing of my thesis and how consensus on the final version of the thesis will be reached. My two supervisors are so organized and efficient that I really feel embarrassed and guilty if I do not achieve the set milestones as per the agreed timeframe. They give me such clear and constructive feedback that enable me to understand my areas of weakness and how I could fix them…...their feedback makes me think critically. Even when I had to go back to my country when my father passed away in my first year of my studies they were very supportive. When my mother also passed on the following year, I was devastated and had to go back to my country again but they encouraged me to be strong and to persevere through the hardships. Were it not for their encouragement I would have given up my PhD studies at that point. Now I am determined to complete my studies come what may!', declared Nexus.

Discussion

On one hand, the case study captures some of the main challenges faced by doctoral students which were identified by Hockey (1994), namely the nature of supervision they experience, the feeling of being isolated and time management. It shows doctoral students convening informal gatherings which create environments that help to tackle the problem of isolation while at the same time providing a platform for frank discussion of personal feelings and experiences. The case study also reveals six doctoral students with different personality attributes and circumstances. Regardless of the nature of possible causes, strained student–supervisor relationships could worsen drop-out rates of PhD students – which is a waste of resources for all stakeholders involved, the students themselves, students' families, supervisors, academic institutions and relevant national institutions such as ministries of higher education.

On the other hand, the case study depicts some challenges which supervisors have to face in dealing with such doctoral students with different backgrounds, needs, personalities and capabilities. The challenges include having to deal with second language-related problems, dynamic student–supervisor relationships, cultural shock in the case of some students, 'technological shock' for some students drawn from relatively under-resourced academic institutions, different performance levels, and factors that may be beyond the control of the supervisor such as family issues, financial matters and immigration issues (in the case of foreign students). It is therefore critical for supervisors to be flexible and 'broad-minded' so as to be able to 'accommodate' scholarly, emotional and socio-economic diversity of the doctoral students they supervise without compromising on the quality of the doctoral graduates they produce. Supervisors aim to develop PhD graduates who are scholars capable of making meaningful contributions to the pool of knowledge shared by the academic community. Whereas some supervisors may realize that such scholarly skills need to be developed and nurtured through systematic training or instruction (Rose and McClafferty, 2001), some may expect their students to achieve these on their own. Such an approach could lead to students struggling with their studies to the extent that student–supervisor relationships may be strained and in some cases, the withdrawal of the student from the doctoral programme.

Student–supervisor relationships depicted by the case study

The case study captures different types of doctoral student–supervisor relationships and different approaches to supervision, which arguably fit into a model of supervision created by Gatfield (2005). The model takes into account structural aspects of supervision on one hand and support provided to students by the supervisor on the other. Gatfield (2005) describes the extreme end of the support component as being 'pastoral' style of supervision. The structural aspect ranges from a low level characterized by lack of any milestones and deadlines to the high level of structure characterized by well-defined millstones with strict timeframes. Supervision style that encompasses high levels of both support and defined structure is referred to as 'contractual' type of supervision (Gatfield, 2005).

The case study also gives an insight into some of the views, expectations and frustrations of doctoral students. The personality attributes of students revealed in such 'informal' discussions by students are not likely to be picked up in formal discussions between students and supervisors. The different types of relationships captured are summarized below.

The 'Todd–supervisor' relationship

This relationship shows the dynamics that may occur in a doctoral student–supervisor relationship over a period of time. Although Todd was initially happy with his supervisor, he seems to be currently unhappy with his relationship with his supervisor which he says changed for the worse after he got married and had a family of his own. He contends that he is no longer able to put into his studies as much time as he used to do, but he thinks the supervisor should accept the changes and 'accommodate' them. On the other hand, the supervisor has changed her approach and is now employing a structured supervision style. She may be concerned that if she does not give 'strict' instructions with deadlines Todd may not make meaningful progress in his PhD studies.

Todd has a new identity as a family man with responsibilities which seems to affect his relationship with his supervisor, resulting in the supervisor asserting her 'control' over him. Todd's supervisor was initially 'flexible', without 'enforcing' milestones to be completed within given timeframes, but later changed and became very strict. Thus, according to the supervisory management grid developed by Gatfield (2005), initially the supervision style was more or less 'laissez-faire', with low structure and support, changing to become 'directional', with high structure but still low support.

The 'Fatso–supervisor' relationship

Fatso's supervisor also seems to fall into the same category of supervision style as that of Todd's supervisor. Using an alternative supervision model to that proposed by Gatfield (2005), Todd's and Fatso's supervisors could be considered (perhaps from the point of view of the supervised students) to be using the 'master–slave' or 'apprenticeship' model described by Grant (2008). The 'master–slave' model is characterized by heavy-handedness on the part of the supervisor which induces 'fear' and hence 'obedience' in the student who is analogous to the 'slave'. The focus of the master–slave model are benefits for the supervisor without much consideration for benefits for or interests of the student. The apprenticeship model is centred on acquisition of knowledge and skills by the student with the supervisor as the 'provider'. Unlike the apprenticeship model which ideally should be bi-directional and has potential to be so, the master–slave approach to supervision is based mainly on unidirectional relationships due to power differentials between supervisors and students. The relationship between Fatso and his supervisor demonstrates tensions that may be caused by different expectations between students and supervisors.

Whereas Fatso seems to be eager to get the PhD studies out of the way, his supervisor expects publications and not just a thesis. Potential benefits of publishing do not seem to matter to Fatso. He does not consider publishing his work to be important, hence his dislike of his supervisor. Fatso is against the idea of sacrificing some time for leisure for the sake of his PhD studies. To him, life, with its various forms of fun, should continue regardless of him being engaged in a PhD degree programme. The supervisor applies a strict approach in order to have work done timeously.

The 'Marvellous–supervisor' relationship

Although it is unlikely that any supervisory relationships will be perfect, there are examples of good relationships between doctoral students and their supervisors. Marvellous seems to have a good relationship with her supervisors. It also seems that the two supervisors work well together and agree on work plans upfront. Marvellous argues that if one manages one's time properly, one can be married and also be a successful PhD student. She included her social plans (getting married by end of the the third year of PhD studies) in her overall plan for the PhD programme which she discussed with her supervisors. Marvellous' supervisors use a style that has high structure as well as high support, which makes it a 'contractual' type of supervision according to the model by Gatfield (2005). The style has worked well, and Marvellous' satisfaction is a clear indication of this.

The 'Blazo–supervisor' relationship

Socio-economic factors surrounding doctoral students can affect student–supervisor relationships positively or negatively. Blazo seems to have a good relationship with his supervisor, with a lot of family support from his side as well as from his fiancé's side. Thus, all the stakeholders consider Blazo's PhD studies as being worthwhile and as a good investment for the future. Although Blazo seems to be happy with his supervisor, probably due to a 'pastoral' style of supervision that his supervisor uses, it is not clear from what he tells his peers if the supervisor sets milestones for him. He also has family support, which seems to complement his good relationship with his supervisor.

The 'Warisha–supervisors' relationship

Examples of challenges that could be caused by co-supervision are shown in Warisha–supervisor relationship. It seems that there is a clash of supervision styles, with the primary supervisor using a 'contractual' style, while the co-supervisor uses a 'pastoral' approach. Warisha is happy with his co-supervisor but he thinks that his primary supervisor does not care about his personal life. He also has a problem of some kind of tension between the primary supervisor and the co-supervisor. It seems that there is no framework for the supervision that is agreed on by the two supervisors and the student. Consequently, Warisha has problems with conflicting instructions coming from the two supervisors. Whereas the primary supervisor is focused on academic issues only, the co-supervisor goes out of his way to try and help the student with other non-academic matters such as applying for study permit which can indirectly affect the student's studies negatively if not sorted out.

The 'Nexus–supervisors' relationship

Although Nexus has stayed in the PhD programme for five years, she is quite happy with her supervisors. She has encountered some personal problems during the course of her studies, having lost both her parents one after the other in consecutive years, but the support and encouragement from her two supervisors has kept her determined to complete her PhD studies. However, in countries like South Africa such doctoral students like Nexus who overstay in the university postgraduate system compromise the financial position of universities as government subsidies are based on completion rates. It could be argued that a combination of the 'contractual' and the 'pastoral' styles could result in better progress in terms of completion of PhD studies as Nexus, whose supervisors use a 'pastoral' approach only, has overstayed in the postgraduate system.

Global increase in demand for postgraduates as economies become knowledge driven

There is evidence that economies of most countries globally are increasingly becoming knowledge driven (Bologna process-European Higher Education Area), which leads to an increased demand for postgraduates in general and PhD graduates in particular. Consequently, pressure on institutions and supervisors to improve completion rates is steadily mounting. For instance, in South Africa universities get subsidies for articles published in journals accredited by the Department of Higher Education and Technology and for the graduates they produce annually. Through such incentives, the South African government is making efforts to promote and strengthen tertiary education, especially at postgraduate level. The emphasis on postgraduate studies has been explicitly stated at policy level in the National Development Plan which states that South Africa aims to 'Increase the percentage of PhD qualified staff in the higher education sector from the current 34% to over 75% by 2030' and 'Produce more than 100 doctoral graduates per million per year by 2030. That implies an increase from 1420 in 2010 to well over 5 000 a year' (National Development Plan 2030-Executive Summary). Working under such pressure, supervisors may find it difficult to 'accommodate' or take care of social and or emotional challenges of their students, leading to strained relationships as depicted by the relationship between Todd and Fatso and their respective supervisors.

As the numbers of doctoral students enrolled increases, research is increasingly becoming multidisciplinary, leading to some doctoral students having to be supervised by more than one supervisor. Consequently, student–supervisor relationships are inevitably becoming more complex as primary and co-supervisors may have different supervision styles and personality attributes. Thus, instead of leading to a wider collegial environment for the students, co-supervision may lead to tensions in the student–supervisor relationship and may also cause divergent supervisory guidance which confuses the student. As depicted by the 'Warisha–supervisors' type of relationship in the case study, students may suffer quietly without even alerting the relevant university structures about their challenges, let alone discussing the issues with the supervisors concerned.

Whereas doctoral students may try to tackle the problem of isolation through their own informal gatherings, supervisors could use group supervisory approaches to try and mitigate the problem of doctoral students feeling isolated and lonely. The group approach enables peer interactions which promote participatory learning (Gardner, 2008; Lovitts, 2008; Warhurst, 2006) on one hand while potentially helping to dissipate some tensions in interpersonal relationships on the other. In order to take care of different needs of different students, the group supervisory approach should be complemented with one-on-one supervisory sessions tailor-made for specific students.

Developing knowledge and skills

As students enrolling for postgraduate studies at a particular university are drawn from different universities with different educational qualities, supervisors should not assume that postgraduate students have the same levels of knowledge and skills when they embark on their PhD studies. Taber (2001) points out that such assumptions could lead to learning impediments, which in turn could negatively affect the relationships between students and their supervisors. According to Franke and Arvidsson (2011), supervision should be composed of two main components, a knowledge component as well as a relational component. It is therefore critical for supervisors to assess the needs of each student, and to discuss interventional activities with the specific students from the outset. Various authors have recommended that supervisors should play an active role in teaching their students research and mentoring them (Pearson and Brew, 2002; Price and Money, 2002; Manathunga, 2005) rather than a passive approach based on an assumption that the students already have research capabilities (Johnson et al. 2000). However, it does not necessarily mean that the supervisors themselves have to always teach or train the students; most universities have postgraduate support programmes which are very useful in terms of developing knowledge and skills. The support programmes complement the inputs and guidance provided by the supervisors.

Supervisors have to draw up a plan of all the workshops, courses, tutorials, readings, etc. which their students have to undertake in a given timeframe. The aim should be to facilitate the three stages in the PhD programme, namely (i) development and writing of research proposals, (ii) data collection and analysis and (iii) thesis writing as well as publishing research findings. Thow and Murray (2001) emphasize the need for supervisors to guide the student during the writing phase. The guidance should enable the students not only to write up their PhD thesis but to write and publish articles based on their research projects. Universities are increasingly expecting PhD students to publish at least 3 papers by the time they graduate. As the supervisors guide the students, it is important to strike a balance between the need to provide support and the need to develop a resourceful researcher who can independently think critically (Gurr 2001).

Effect of the quality of feedback on student–supervisor relationship

One of the most important interactions between students and supervisors is in the form of feedback on work submitted to supervisors by the students. Thus, the quality of feedback has great potential to determine the effectiveness of teaching and learning during the course of the postgraduate programme (Hyland and Tse, 2004; Hattie and Timperley, 2007; Kumar and Stracke, 2007). Supervisors use the pieces of work submitted by students to assess comprehension of concepts as well as ability to write clearly and logically. The pieces of work also help supervisors to break down complex tasks into small steps which should be achieved within given timeframes, thus 'setting the pace' for the students. On the other hand, feedback from supervisors is critical for students to know how well they are progressing and which areas they need to strengthen.

Feedback should enlighten the student so as to understand in what way his or her piece of work could be improved. The supervisor should unpack the student's work in order to highlight any strengths and any weaknesses. The student may not have retained pertinent fundamental concepts or subject content, or may have retained them but without understanding them well enough to apply them to a given task or to use them to develop appropriate theories or hypotheses. Thus, feedback should not be merely negative comments which do not help the student to rectify any weaknesses.

Latent gender issues

Controversial debate on gender issues is sparked off by the statement 'It can work for you because you are a lady and once you get married your husband will support you adequately and you can continue with your studies' which is made by Todd. Fatso supports this point of view, which implies that unlike male PhD students, female students can manage to undertake PhD studies even when they are married because their husbands take care of them. However, that insinuation is countered by the fact that Blazo's fiancé is fending not only for herself and her two children, but also for Blazo, the father of the children who is a full-time PhD student. Another dimension of the gender issue is the possible strain that may be caused by the need for female PhD students to go on maternity leave if they become pregnant during the course of their PhD programmes. It means that if postgraduate supervisors do not know how best to handle such gender-related issues the student–supervisor relationship may be compromised.

In supporting Todd, Fatso goes further to insinuate that female PhD students are favoured by supervisors, a view which is discredited by Marvellous for lack of supporting evidence. Gender issues and perceptions which have affected other social areas such as the work place are bound to affect learning and teaching in higher education. Although Johnson and Green (2000) alluded to the issue of gender (2000), there is a paucity of research and literature on how gender-related issues play out in postgraduate supervision in general and student–supervisor relationships in particular. For instance, whereas labour laws and institutional policies give details of maternity and paternity leave for employees, there is limited clarity as to how PhD students should be handled. In addition, there are limited empirical data on whether or not gender of students and or of supervisors influences firstly choice of students or supervisors and secondly student–supervisor relationship.

Fatso's views regarding female students captures perceptions which may affect student–supervisor relationships as supervisors may be conscious of the perceptions hence may hesitate to act in certain ways for fear of being seen as being biased on the basis of gender. For instance, a supervisor may hesitate to be supportive to a student lest the support is perceived as being gender-based favouritism. On the other hand, taking a structured approach with strict milestones could mistakenly be perceived as deliberate gender-based action to make life difficult for a student.

Dealing with emotional challenges in student–supervisor relationships

The case study shows that PhD students may have to deal with difficult emotional challenges just like any other people in the real world. Nexus had to deal with the loss of her parents and she got emotional support from her supervisors. Even if Nexus has overstayed in the PhD programme, it is not anybody's fault because death of family members is beyond anybody's control and is inevitable. Most situations that cause emotional challenges cannot be anticipated in advance; hence when they occur they may disrupt planned activities which may lead to some deadlines and milestones being missed. It is such situations which highlight the tension that supervisors may have to deal with; on one hand they have to be supportive and 'pastoral', while on the other hand they have to ensure that their students achieve their main objective of being in the PhD programme, which is to successfully obtain their degree.

As shown in the case study, appreciation of emotional support given by supervisors may result in strengthened relationship which may encourage the student to persevere in his or her PhD studies against all odds. It is better to at least have a PhD student who takes long to complete his/her studies than to have a student who gives up and terminates the studies prematurely. Also captured in the case study are other emotional challenges such as illnesses of close relatives.

Co-supervision

Student–supervisor relationships are more complicated if there is more than one supervisor involved. As depicted in the case of Warisha, the different supervisors may have different styles of supervision, and may operate without a clear supervision 'framework' agreed upon right from the beginning. The supervision framework helps to outline milestones for the student, roles of each supervisor, details of how and what the student should submit to each supervisor, whether supervisors give feedback to the student separately (as is the case in Warisha's case) or the supervisors consolidate their feedback before giving consolidated feedback to the student. Another approach is for the supervisors to be responsible for different aspects of the student's research project as well as the ensuing write-up.

Concluding remarks

Postgraduate supervision requires a combination of pedagogical knowledge and personal relationship skills on the part of supervisors. It also requires ability to be pragmatic so as to accommodate different students with different needs. In spite of all these differences at the entry point and during the actual postgraduate programme, the quality of the final products should meet some acceptable minimum standards in terms of the graduates produced. Thus, supervisors have the task of ensuring some level of institutional and probably national uniformity in terms of the quality of the postgraduates they produce, regardless of the different qualities of students entering into the postgraduate degree programmes.

In light of the differences in characteristics and backgrounds of students, this chapter argues for a holistic and pragmatic approach to postgraduate supervision rather than a 'one-size-fits-all' approach in order to take care of the different needs and capabilities of the students. Factors that could potentially affect the student–supervisor relationship and may lead to the need for proactive pragmatism in supervision style include level of prior knowledge and skills, intellectual capability, marital status, financial circumstances, whether one is local or foreign student, whether there is co-supervision or not and arguably gender-related issues.

References

Bartlett, A., and Mercer, G. (2000). Reconceptualising discourses of power in postgraduate pedagogies. Teac. High. Educ. 5(2), 195–204.
Bologna process-European Higher Education Area. Available at: http://www.ehea.info/ (accessed 23 August 2017).
Franke, A., and Arvidsson, B. (2011). Research supervisors' different ways of experiencing supervision of doctoral students. Stud. Higher Educ. 36(1), 7–19.
Gardner, S.K. (2008). 'What's too much and what's too little?': The process of becoming an independent researcher in Doctoral Education. The Journal of Higher Education 79(3), 327–350.

Gatfield, T. (2005). An investigation into PhD supervisory management styles: development of a dynamic conceptual model and its managerial implications. Journal of Higher Education Policy and Management, 27(3), 311–325.

Golde, C.M. (2000). Should I stay or should I go? Student descriptions of the doctoral attrition process. The Review of Higher Education 23(2), 99–227.

Grant, B.M. (2008). Agonistic struggle: master–slave dialogues in humanities supervision. Arts and Humanities in Higher Education 7(1), 9–27.

Gurr, G. (2001). Negotiating the 'rackety bridge': a dynamic model for aligning supervisory style with research student development. High. Educ. Res. Dev. 20(1), 81–92.

Hattie, J., and Timperley, H. (2007). The power of feedback. Review of Educational Research, 77(1), 81–112.

Hayland, K., and Tse, P. (2004). Metadiscourse in academic writing: A reappraisal. Applied Linguistics, 25(2), 156–177.

Hockey, J. (1994). New Territory: problems of adjusting to the first year of a social science PhD. Stud. Higher Educ. 19(2), 177–190.

Ives, G., and Rowley, G. (2005). Supervisor selection or allocation and continuity of supervision: PhD students' progress and outcomes. Stud. Higher Educ. 30(5), 535–555.

Johnson, L., Lee, A., and Green, B. (2000). The PhD and the autonomous self: Gender, rationality and postgraduate pedagogy. Stud. Higher Educ. 25(2), 135–147.

Kumar, V., and Stracke, E. (2007). An analysis of written feedback on a PhD thesis. Teaching in Higer Education, 12(4), 461–470.

Li, S., and Searle, C. (2007). Managing criticism in PhD supervision: A qualitative case study. Stud. Higher Educ. 32(4), 511–526.

Lovitts, B. (2008). The transition to independent research: Who makes it, who does not and why? The Journal of Higher Education 79(3), 296–325.

Manathunga, C. (2005). Early warning signs in postgraduate research education: a different approach to timely completions. Teaching in Higher Education 10(2), 223–237.

Manathunga, C. (2007). Supervision as mentoring: the role of power and boundary crossing. Stud. Contin. Educ. 29(2), 207–221.

Marsh, H.W., Rowe, K.J., and Martin, A. (2002). PhD students' evaluations of research supervision. The Journal of Higher Education 73(3). 313–348.

Murphy, N., Bain, J.D., and Conrad, L.M. (2007). Orientations to research higher degree supervision. High. Educ. 53(2), 209–234.

National Development Plan 2030 (Executive Summary). Available at: http://www.education.gov.za/LinkClick.aspx?fileticket=09T%2BvV0a5Sg%3D&tabid=628&mid=2062 (accessed 23 August 2017).

Pearson, M. (1996). Professionalising PhD education to enhance the quality of the student experience. High. Educ. 32(3), 303–320.

Pearson, M., and Brew, A. (2002). Research training and supervision development. Stud. Higher Educ. 27(2), 135–150.

Price, D., and Money, A. (2002). Alternative models for doctoral mentor organisation and research supervision. Mentoring and Tutoring 10(2), 127–136.

Rose, M., and McClafferty, K. (2001). A call for the teaching of writing in graduate education. Educ. Researcher, 30(2), 27–33.

Taber, K. (2001). The mismatch between assumed prior knowledge and the learner's conceptions: A typology of learning impediments. Educ. Stud. 27(2), 159–171.

Thow, M.K., and Murray, R. (2001). Facilitating student writing during project supervision. Physiotherapy 87(3), 134–139.

Warhurst, R.P. (2006). 'We really felt part of something': Participatory learning amongst peers within a university teaching development community of practice. International Journal for Academic Development, 11(2), 111–122.

Index

A

Abductive research approach 14
Accreditation 5
Accredited taught programme 2
Activity plan 66
Adult learning theories 9, 15
Aesthetic values 11
Alder Hey scandal 80
Animal ethics committees 64
Appendices 66, 75
Application of knowledge 3
Area of specialization 3
Associate degree 25
Authorship issues 85
Axiology 9, 11

B

Behaviourism theory 15
Being and becoming 17
Belmont Report 80
Budget 65

C

Career goals 2
Career path 2
Case study: 'Guys! Let me tell you about my PhD supervisor' 98
Categorical variables 36
Causal questions 29
Chapters 71
    chapter 1: introduction 73
    chapter 2: literature review 73
    chapter 3: methods 73
    chapter 4: results 74
    chapter 5: discussion 74
    chapter 6: conclusion 74
Characteristics of learners 9, 17
Cluster sampling technique 63
Cognitive learning theory 16
Comparative questions 28
Computers 6
Conceptual framework 60

Concurrent criterion validity 45
Conflict of interest 85
Consequentialism 11
Construct validity 43
Constructivism 13
Content validity 43
Continuous variables 36
Continuum of control in research 33
Convenient sampling technique 63
Cosmology 10
Co-supervision 107
Council for International Organizations of Medical Sciences (CIOMS) 80
Courses 6
Criteria for selecting eligible authors 85
Criterion validity 44
Critical appraisal of literature 54

D

Data analysis and interpretation 63
Data collection methods and procedures 63
Dealing with emotional challenges in student–supervisor relationships 106
Deciding to obtain postgraduate qualification 1
Declaration of Helsinki 80
Deductive research approach 14
Definition of professional doctorate degree 94
Deontology 11
Descriptive research questions 28
Developing knowledge and skills 104
Dissertations 70
Doctor of Philosophy degrees 22
Doctorate degrees 3, 21
Doctors 20
Double-dipping 87

E

Effect of the quality of feedback on student–supervisor relationship 105
Empiricism 14
Entry requirements for postgraduate studies 26
Environment in which research is conducted 89
Epistemology 9, 11
Ethical issues 64, 84
Ethical or moral values 11
Ethnography 32
European Qualifications Framework (EQF) 24
Examination 95
Examples of some 'subjective' variables 35
Examples of some 'tangible' variables 35
Experimental research 32

F

Fabrication of data 81
Face validity 41
Falsification of data 82
Feasibility 6
Final write-up 3
Flow from topic to conclusion 77

Formats of theses, dissertations and research reports 71
    conventional monograph 71
    publication format 75
    submissible manuscript format 77
Framework for Higher Education Qualification (FHEQ) 24
Full-time postgraduate programmes 6
Fundamental components of research proposal 50
    title 50
    introduction 50
    statement of the problem 52
    research question and/or hypothesis 52
    aim or main objective of the study 53
    specific objectives 53
    literature review 54
    research methodology 61
Fundamental ethical principles 64
Fundamental steps common to all types of literature review 56
Funding/grant-related misconducts 87

G

General structure of a conventional monograph 71
General structure of introduction section 52
General structure of professional doctorate degrees 94
Grading systems 25
Graduate Record Examination (GRE) 26
Grounded theory approach 31

H

Honorary doctorate degree 22
Honours degrees 19, 20
Human ethics committees 64

I

Inductive research approach 14
Inferential statistics 64
Informed consent 85
Integrative literature review 54
Intellectual property rights and patents 89
Internal consistency reliability 41
Interpretivism 12
Inter-rater reliability 41
Intra-rater reliability 41
Issues pertaining to collaboration 88

L

Laptops 6
Latent gender issues 105
Learning at university level 9
Lecturers 1
Levels of academic programmes 24

M

Master of Philosophy degrees 21
Master's degrees 3, 21
Meta-analysis 55
Metaphysics 10

Meta-synthesis 56
Methodological issues 82
Minimum credits 6
Misappropriation of funds 87
Modes of delivery 4, 6
    face to face 4
    flipped classroom 4
    problem-based learning 4
    work-based learning 5
    e-learning 5
    distance education 5
    blended learning 5
Modules 6
Multi-stage sampling technique 63

N

Narrative literature review 54
Naturalistic observational research 30
Not accounting for research grants through reports 87
Not so obvious dimensions of research integrity 85
Notional hours and credits 23
Nuremburg code 80

O

Observational research 30
On-the-job experience 3
Ontology 9, 10
Over-researching certain communities or geographical locations 90

P

Parasitic collaborators 88
Partial disclosure of information to prospective participants 81
Participant observational research 31
Part-time postgraduate programmes 6
Phenomenology 32
Philosophical background of knowledge 9
Philosophical concepts 9
Philosophical jargon 9
Plagiarism 83
Positivism 12
Postdictive criterion validity 45
Postgraduate diploma qualification 3
Postgraduate diplomas and certificates 23
Postgraduate honours degree 3, 20
Postgraduate programmes 19
Postgraduate qualification 1
Postgraduate studies 1
Postgraduate thesis, dissertation or research report 69
Post-positivism 13
Post-study issues 90
Potential challenges: completion rates and attrition risks 96
Power differentials 88
Pragmatism 13
Predictive criterion validity 44
Probability sampling techniques 62
Professional doctorate degree 22, 93

Professional postgraduate qualifications 3
Publishing same data more than once 87
Purposive sampling technique 63

Q

Qualitative research 31

R

Random sampling 62
Rationalism 14
Reasons for obtaining postgraduate qualifications 2
References 66
References, reference styles and reference management software 75
Relational questions 29
Reliability and validity of quantitative research instruments 39, 46
Requirements for enrolment into postgraduate studies 24
Research approaches 14
Research capacity 9
Research design 61
Research integrity: the obvious and the less obvious dimensions 79
Research methodology 61
Research paradigms 9, 12
Research projects 2, 3, 6
Research proposal template 51
Research question and hypothesis 28
Research reports 71
Research-based postgraduate qualifications 3

S

Search engines and databases 57
Searching for relevant literature and choice of search words 56
Selecting and organizing literature that has to be read in detail 57
Sequencing of courses or modules 6
Setting research agenda 90
Sharing of specimens and data 88
Social constructivism 13
Social contract theory 11
South African National Qualification Framework (NQF) 24
South African Qualification Authority (SAQA) 24
Stationary 6
Stratified random sampling 62
Student-centred learning 9
Students 1
Student–supervisor relationships depicted by the case study 101
Supervision 95
Synthesising literature into a coherent appraisal: the five Cs 58
    citing 58
    comparing and contrasting 58
    critiquing and connecting 58
Systematic literature review 55
Systematic sampling 62

T

Target population, sampling technique and sample size 61
Taught plus research postgraduate qualifications 3
Taught postgraduate qualifications 2

Teaching approaches 9
Teleology 11
Terminology 70
Test–retest reliability 40
The principle of autonomy 64
The principle of beneficence 64
The principle of justice 65
The principle of non-maleficence 65
The triple R principle 84
Theoretical framework 60
Thesis 70
Thesis formats 95
Time management 6
Training by librarians 59
Transformative learning theory 16
Trovan clinical trial 80
Tuition fees and other costs 6
Tuskegee scandal 80
Types of literature review 54
Types of reliability of quantitative instruments 40
Types of research 29
Types of validity of quantitative instruments 41
Types of variables 36

U

Undergraduate degree programmes 25
Undergraduate Honours degree 20
Undergraduate studies 1
Utilitarianism 11

V

Variables 34

W

What is research? 27
Writing a research proposal 49

www.ingramcontent.com/pod-product-compliance
Lightning Source LLC
Chambersburg PA
CBHW071002080526
44587CB00015B/2316